# Thelma & Louise
## and
# Something to Talk About

# Thelma & Louise
# and
# Something to Talk About

### Screenplays by

## Callie Khouri

**Grove Press**
*New York*

*Published simultaneously in Canada*
*Printed in the United States of America*

Library of Congress Cataloging-in-Publication Data
Khouri, Callie.
    [Thelma & Louise]
    Thelma & Louise; and, Something to talk about: screenplays / by
  Callie Khouri.
      p.    cm.
    ISBN 0-8021-3462-9
    1. Motion picture plays.    I. Khouri, Callie. Something to talk
about. 1966.    II. Something to talk about.    III. Title.
PS3561.H58T48    1996
791.43'72—dc20                         96-1704

Design by Laura Hammond Hough

Grove Press

00 01  10 9 8 7 6 5 4

# Contents

# An Interview with Callie Khouri

With the success of *Thelma & Louise* and *Something to Talk About,* Callie Khouri is redefining the way women are perceived on screen. Her scripts continue to send shock waves through Hollywood, not only because of their flawless construction and rich, nuanced dialogue, but because the female characters who drift, ramble, shoot, cheat, kill, suffer, whine, light up, and pound tequila through them defy the conventional stereotypes of women on screen. They are not good girls or bad girls, angels or whores. They are not sex objects or sex victims, or corpses left in the wake of a crazed serial killer. Callie Khouri digs her characters out of the narrow tombs of tradition. She unearths their stories from her imagination as a scientist in a desert digs up bones. She breathes life into them and makes them our heroes. And in doing so, she captures not only the power of women, but our attention—and sometimes even our hearts.

*Where did you grow up?*
I grew up in Paducah, Kentucky, and lived there till I was seventeen. I moved there from Texas when I was six and then left and went to

college at Purdue University. I imagine it's pretty Republican now, but at the time, it was trying to be liberal, just like every other place in the mid-seventies.

*Did you know Amelia Earhart used to teach there?*
No! It just figures they wouldn't play that aspect of it up! That's probably not the only thing that got by me. I was a drama major at a major ag-and-engineering school. Not too bright. I went there because for about ten seconds I was going to be a landscape architect. Instead I ended up studying acting. Of course, I didn't graduate.

*So after Purdue you moved to Hollywood?*
No, I moved to Nashville and lived there for a few years, and then I moved to L.A.

*What did you do in Nashville?*
I studied acting intermittently. I waitressed. I worked at a regional theater there, till it closed. I received a CETA grant. I was federally funded to study acting. Ha ha, Jesse Helms. Then I moved to L.A. because I just ran out of stuff to do there. And I wasn't in the music business. And that was like being in L.A. and not being in the entertainment business. Everybody's doing one thing, and you want to be doing it, too. But I don't have any musical talent, so there wasn't any reason to stay. I can play the radio.

*What happened when you moved to L.A.?*
I studied acting at the Strasberg Institute for a while and with Peggy Feury. And then in 1985, I quit. I just couldn't stand it anymore. I realized I was never going to get a job. It just wasn't going to happen. And when it's not going to happen, there's no consolation, no solace. Ever. And you know, I waited as long as I could, because I did really love acting, although I have no desire to do it now. But then I realized I'd spent the last ten years on something that was never going to pan out and I was going to have to do something else. So I ended up getting a job at a production company. As a receptionist. I had to promise that I would never try to move up into production, that I

would stay and answer the phone and nothing else, which of course I swore on my life was my highest ambition. They produced commercials and music videos. Once I figured out what was going on, of course, I moved into production. I started as a runner, and then a P.A., and then a production coordinator, and then a production manager, until I was producing. This took about a year. I produced mainly music videos, which was grueling work but was a great learning experience. And then I figured it out. I figured out that there were all these people writing scripts without a shred of discernible talent. And they were getting movies made. And I just thought, "You know, I can do better than that."

*Were you reading a lot of scripts?*
Not a lot, but some. But just going to movies and hearing the things that came out of actors' mouths. And I thought, "I'll write a screenplay and see if I can finish it." The screenplay was *Thelma & Louise*.

*How did you get that idea?*
My favorite question. I sent away for it. Actually, I was driving home late one night from the set of some music video, and I pulled up in front of my house and thought, "Two women go on a crime spree." That was the idea for *Thelma & Louise*. I started developing it from there. Why would two women go on a crime spree? Why would *I* go on a crime spree? And the other thing is, I had the image of the car flying into the Grand Canyon. So I knew that's where it was going. In some kind of strange flash, I saw their journey, not the actual physical journey, but how they would start out and what they would become. I should say I *felt* it. Generally, when I write, I start with the feeling first, and then the idea comes later to support that feeling.

*And what was that feeling with* Thelma & Louise *?*
Just that feeling of wanting to bust out, you know?

*Wanting to bust out of being a music video producer?*
I wanted to bust out of my life. Really, really badly. I was just at a place where I wasn't happy, I wasn't creatively fulfilled in any way, and I

just wasn't who I wanted to be. I wasn't essentially who I am. I was the product of a lot of wasted years and bad relationships and ennui and frustration at not really knowing what I wanted to do. And I just wanted out of that. And I got out.

*In a big way.*
Yeah, fortunately, they gave me a ride out of there. Plus, to this day, writing that script was the most fun I've ever had in my life.

*How long did it take you?*
Six months. Because I was working on music videos the whole time. It was just so much fun because I knew it was going to be good. To me, I mean. Whether it was to anybody else, I didn't know. I didn't even care. I never thought about it in terms of "How viable is it going to be in the marketplace?" I just thought, "Somebody is going to read this thing and just go, 'Oh my God.'"

*How did you learn the format?*
I just looked at other scripts. The structure was apparent. Very linear and simple. There are little things—like when Thelma robs the store, where she's telling what just happened in the past and it's being shown in the future, where the guys are watching it on video the next day—that just kind of happened along the way.

*That's pretty complex.*
I wanted to figure out some way to take it out of real time. It wouldn't have been as funny if you'd seen her doing it. It was just more visually interesting to show it through the video camera and it accomplished more in terms of setting her up as a real outlaw. And it was just funnier.

*Who was the first person you showed it to when you finished?*
My friend Amanda Temple. I wanted to direct it, and I wanted her to produce it with me. We had worked together a lot producing videos for her husband, director Julien Temple, and I really wanted her to

do it with me. We started showing it around a little bit, trying to figure out what low-budget companies would want to make a film like that with a first-time director.

*What was the initial response to the material?*
Mixed. You know, a lot of chicken-shit "What are you going to do about that ending?" "Why does she have to shoot him and kill him? Wouldn't she be more likable if she shot him in the leg?" That kind of thing.

*What kind of coverage did the script get?*
Some of it was really good. Really complimentary. Some just didn't get it at all. One studio's coverage said, "A story about two sisters . . ." and I'm just thinking, "Start over. You idiot." I should have saved that. But I *so* didn't care. There was no way I was going to take no for an answer. By that time, I'd watched so many talentless producers and directors get movies made that I knew we could do this. It wasn't a matter of being allowed to. There was just no way this wasn't going to happen. Anything can happen if you make it happen. It doesn't matter what it is. Look at all the crappy movies that get made. Somebody makes that happen. It's not just luck. It's not because the movies are so good. It's because they go out and they find someone they can rook into putting up the dough for it. I knew I could be convincing enough to find that one person.

*How did you get the script to Ridley Scott?*
Amanda Temple gave it to Mimi Polk, who was working with Ridley, to see if she would have any ideas about financing. Mimi really liked it and asked if it would be okay if Ridley read it. He did, and we had a couple of meetings, and they said, "What if we produce it?" I talked to Amanda about it, who—besides having just found out that she was pregnant with their first child—thought that I should do it because it would most certainly get made. Right now. And I knew I was looking at years and years of doing this if I was going to try to direct it myself. It was the bird in the hand decision.

*Did Ridley make it clear that you would not be able to direct it?*
Well, let's just say the idea didn't seem to generate a lot of enthusiasm at first. They said they were going to talk to other directors, and I said, "I want to be on that list."

*What did they say? Did you have a reel?*
They didn't really say much. They didn't know me. They showed it to a lot of directors, and once they started getting into the B-list, then I started going, "Okay, fuck this, I should be doing it." I mean they were talking to directors that were saying, "Hey, here's a great idea. Let's have Louise have had an affair with Darryl sometime in the past!" And I'm thinking, "I'd rather fucking burn it."

*How did Ridley come around to deciding he wanted to direct it?*
We had spent a lot of time talking about the script, and other directors were really starting to get interested. But after months and months of talking about it, it just became, in my mind, a foregone conclusion that Ridley would direct it. I think it would have been impossible for him to *let* someone else do it, and I didn't really want anybody else to do it.

*Did they offer it to any women directors?*
No. And I was saying, "Hey, if you want a woman to direct it, I want to do it. Don't give it to some other woman who didn't fucking write it and doesn't have any attachment to it and needs a commercial movie."

*Did you have to do another polish with Ridley?*
Yes, but it was so minimal it didn't really feel like work.

*What about when the cast came on? Did you have to make adjustments?*
Well, there were some things that clearly needed adjusting. For instance, Susan Sarandon was older than the character that I wrote, so adjustments had to be made for that. In the original draft, the relationship between Louise and Jimmy was different. She was younger, so when they got together, there was this hopefulness there. It wasn't

so much her saying, "No, this isn't ever going to happen." She did say no, but they went through this mock wedding ceremony in their motel room where they just kind of made promises to each other. But it was really sad and sweet.

*That melancholy sort of came through in the version that ended up on the screen.*
Mostly the script stayed the same. Things happened when they were shooting. Some scenes were added. The scene where Louise trades all her jewelry for the old man's hat, the scene where she stops the car in the desert in the middle of the night, and of course the Rastafarian on the bike were all their ideas. And there were scenes that didn't make it into the final cut of the movie.

*Is there any scene that you really miss?*
Yeah, there are a couple. But they're scenes that only I would miss, really. There was one scene where Thelma asked Louise, "What really scares you?" And Louise says, "Getting old. Livin' in some tiny apartment with one of those little dogs." And they go through this whole thing about what kind of little dog. And then Louise asks Thelma the same question and she says, "Getting old with Darryl. I just don't think he's gonna be very nice about it." And Louise says, "Well, you don't have to worry about it now." And they just go on.

*Did they film it?*
I don't know if they did or not. And there was another scene about women's prison and Linda Blair in this TV movie called *Born Innocent*, I think.

*I've never seen it.*
It's unbelievable. The gist of it is that she gets raped in prison by all these other girls with a broom handle or some god-awful thing like that. It's hideous. But Thelma and Louise have a conversation about the movie, and you know that they would rather die than get caught and go to women's prison. It really makes you understand exactly what

is going through their minds, and it was funny. But I don't think they even shot it.

*I remember watching* Thelma & Louise *and thinking, "I don't know how this is going to end," because these women are so different now. Why does their newly won independence have to result in suicide?*

It always struck me as preposterous that people saw it as a suicide. I don't even think of them as dead. I just wasn't in any way prepared for people to say, "God, they killed themselves? What kind of message is that?" I want to say, "It's the message *you* came up with, not me." To me, the ending was symbolic, not literal. I mean, come on, read a book. We did everything possible to make sure that you didn't see a literal death. That you didn't see the car land, you didn't see a big puff of smoke come up out of the canyon. You were left with the image of them flying. They flew away, out of this world and into the mass unconscious. Women who are completely free from all the shackles that restrain them have no place in this world. The world is not big enough to support them. They will be brought down if they stay here. They weren't going to be brought down. So let them go. I loved that ending and I loved the imagery. After all they went through I didn't want anybody to be able to touch them. And I think for all the people who say, "What's that saying? Women have got to kill themselves if they want to be strong?" All I have to say is see it again. I think you should see it again.

*Why did these characters create such an uproar when this movie was released?*

I'm not sure that there's one simple reason. But one thing I think is some people really don't like to see women fight back against behavior that is status quo. Society would come completely unglued if women really started responding in kind to the negative stimulus that they deal with every day. If you rewrote *Thelma & Louise* and decided to have a guy come and save Thelma, there wouldn't have been any uproar. If a guy caught another guy raping a woman and killed the rapist, you wouldn't even comment on that. But I mean, some people talk about the blowing up of the truck as a violent act.

*But you even took the driver out.*
I know. It's just a demonstration of how irrational some of the criticism was. For that to be labeled violent when that same summer *Terminator 2* is being lauded for being so pacifist for shooting all the cops in the knees instead of killing them, it was just mind-boggling.

*After* Thelma & Louise *was released, some critics accused you of being uncharitable toward men. Would you say that your depictions of male characters were unflattering?*
Possibly with the characters who were meant to be villains, like the rapist and the truck driver. But overall I think I am certainly not showing anything like the animals you're likely to see in a movie by Martin Scorsese, Francis Ford Coppola, Quentin Tarantino, or Oliver Stone. I've never approached anything as unflattering to men as what they serve up on a regular basis. It's funny, but I've yet to hear any of those guys being criticized for portraying men in a negative way. Quite the opposite. You can show the most low-life, scum-fucking sicko in the world doing all kinds of violent shit to each other, or to women, and nobody says boo. But you have a woman point out that a guy is a sick fuck and blow up his truck, or have a good time with a guy they already kind of know is not on the up-and-up, and all hell breaks loose. I don't know. They overreacted.

*Still others have labeled you a toxic feminist. What do you have to say in response to that?*
Kiss my ass. Kiss my ass. I was raised in this society. Let them get their deal worked out about the way women are treated in films before they start hassling me about the way men are treated. There's a whole genre of films known as "exploitation" based on the degradation of women and a whole bunch of redneck critics extolling its virtues, and until there's a subgenre of women doing the same thing to men in numbers too numerous to count, as is the case with exploitation films, then just shut the fuck up. They only criticize me because I'm a woman, the same way they only criticize Spike Lee and other black filmmakers because they're black. Only women and minorities are under this directive to present responsible role models in nonthreat-

ening, nonviolent movies. All other white guys can do whatever they want. It's just ridiculous.

*Do you feel that you were given a raw deal?*
Well, on one hand yes. On the other hand I have an Oscar sitting on my shelf at home.

*Where do you keep it?*
In my office at home. I keep the blue bag over it that it comes back from the engraver in, so I don't have to look at it every day.

*Why don't you want to look at it?*
I don't know. I don't want the pressure. It was fun though, and I'm glad I have it. I'm very grateful.

*Oftentimes writers who have a certain fluency with characters and dialogue are sometimes weaker on plot and structure. Is that something that you struggle with?*
I struggled with it a lot more in *Something to Talk About. Thelma & Louise* was such a great structure because it was so easy, so linear. You can have people having meaningful conversations screaming down the road at 120 miles per hour. It's the best of both worlds. But a story that's all character driven, with no events to propel it, other than what happens emotionally, is just a lot harder to write. I had a lot of trouble on the second script because of that.

*How did you work through it?*
Well, I spent a lot of time talking to my producers, Paula Weinstein and Anthea Sylbert, and I had a really good friend, Mel Bourdeaux, who helped me a lot. I also hired a wonderful guy named Jim Rogers, who's almost a structure shrink to come in and help me. And basically, I just macheted my way through it.

*So far you've worked within the studio system. How do you feel about the process of script development? Do you respond well to studio notes?*
No, I don't really. Look, some of the people are really great, really

smart. But some aren't, and they have no loyalty to the story or the characters or anything. To them, it's just a marketing endeavor. And to me, it's an artistic endeavor. And those things do not necessarily mesh together in a way that's beneficial to either party. An *Ace Ventura* movie is a marketing dream. But I'm not ever going to write those kinds of movies. That's not what I'm going to be doing with my life. I'm not saying that there's anything wrong with them. Maybe if I could write that way I would. I think they're funny. It's just not what I have a facility for. I have a strong emotional attachment to the characters I write and to the stories I'm trying to tell. So when I have somebody at a studio whose background is in say, accounting, tell me, "Well, we think it should be like this," there's a voice in my head saying, "What do you know? The most creative decision you've made all week is picking your tie. If you think you know so much about creative things, how 'bout letting me run the studio for a week. And spend money where I think it should be spent." That would never happen in a million years, where the artist would get to administrate. But administrators get to tell writers and directors and actors what to do all the time. And they're guessing. They really don't know. And I think I deserve better than somebody's best guess. I have put the time in. Why not go with my best guess? Because before I thought this story up, there was nothing.

*You're writing a script for James L. Brooks at Gracie Films next?*
Yes, and I'm really looking forward to it. I have a two-picture deal there. I just respect Jim so much. This is a guy who is not removed from the difficulty of writing a script. He's slugging it out every day himself. He does not take it lightly. And that's a wonderful quality to have in a producer. Paula Weinstein is another one; even though she's not a writer, she has a great respect and understanding of the writer's process and somehow makes it a little bit easier. She makes you feel that you're not in it alone, even when you are. When I was writing *Something to Talk About,* she would sit there with me till the end of time if I needed her to. She just kept asking questions, trying to unlock doors that I had inadvertently slammed shut through years of struggle with a particular problem.

*How does that process of trying to figure out a story work?*
I have a couple of theories about stories. One is, stories are whole things, like people. You find a story and you have to start digging to uncover it. You may only find one little part at a time, but if it's really a story, all the pieces will be attached. When other people start to get involved, sometimes they'll say, "Well here's an arm. Why don't you hang that on there and use this head,"and you end up with a Frankenstein monster of a story instead of a living, breathing story on its own. We see a lot of those kinds of stories in movie theaters today, stories that are patched together by committee, and that on their own really cannot sustain life. Cannot breathe, cannot impart to you any kind of truth, other than, "It's all bullshit." With me, the story's gotta be completely mine. It has to be something that I'm so committed to telling that I'll just go crazy if I don't get it out. There are plenty of people out there who don't approach it like that. And on some level, I envy that. They just want to write it, get it made, and get it out of their lives and go on to the next thing. I spent four years writing *Something to Talk About*, the hideously titled *Something to Talk About*, which I will now from this point forward refer to as *Grace Under Pressure*, its given title. The true name of that story is *Grace Under Pressure*.

*How did it end up with the title* Something to Talk About*?*
I'm not sure who started it. But the marketing people just decided that somehow that was going to fit the bill. I must say I fought it vehemently because I think it's a stupid title. I love the song, but it had nothing to do with what the movie was about and, as a movie title, seems almost designed to be forgettable. My own mother had a hard time remembering it. Besides, it looked ridiculous on a movie marquee. Asking someone if they want to see *Something to Talk About* sounds like the beginning of an Abbott and Costello routine. And ultimately think it hurt the movie, because it wasn't a title that people can make a connection to. If they weren't going to use the title *Grace Under Pressure*, then we suggested *Saving Grace*, but for reasons that remain a mystery, they were opposed to anything with *Grace* in the title. *Something to Talk About* trivialized it and made it sound like a teen comedy with girls calling each other on the phone. Have I made it clear that I hate it?

*What were some of the other problems that you had to work out with that script? Four years is a long time to spend on one project.*
One of the major problems, it turned out, was with the character of Grace. When I started, it was about a woman who had always aspired to be like her mother. In her mind everything was just fine and she was just doing everything right. All the same events happened as they do in the movie. She saw her husband cheating on her, et cetera. But the events wouldn't propel her to *do* anything. Things just kept *happening to her.* And I just went on like that for years. I just couldn't make the story move forward.

*And what was it?*
It was realizing that if Grace didn't have resistance to who she had become in the first place, if there was not already the seed in her of, "Ugh! This is just proof that I have gone down the wrong road . . ." Her problem was her lack of commitment to her own life and her own decisions, which is ultimately the problem that a lot of women have to deal with anyway. There's no shortage of people who are happily willing to let you give up your own life to do for them. That's always going to be available. The problem comes when you realize that you have no life of your own. And that's the problem that many women end up facing. That is the wall they hit. So I thought, "Why not give her some prior knowledge? And then she has something she can act on."

*And in this case it was the dream of going to veterinary school?*
Yes, which I'd thought was something she'd given up willingly. I realized if I made her not give it up so willingly—if she'd kind of parceled herself away a little at a time, and she kind of used it against her husband and her child—that it was a way of not committing to that and not committing to herself. So that she's always holding back from her husband, she's always holding back from her child, she's always holding back from her career. And she's holding everyone else responsible.

*Because she had been afraid to commit to the one thing she truly wanted to do?*
Yeah, she chickened out. She bailed when she got the chance. You know, I've watched a lot of women do that. To me that was real. That

was something I could get behind. I've heard a lot of women say, "Well, it's not as easy once you have kids." No, it's not. And it's not easy without them either. All the women of my generation have had to watch as our mothers' generation hit that wall of "the kids are gone, now what do we do?" Who are we without that family?

*Answer?*
Well, that's the quest. That's the thing worth figuring out. Who are we without the family, who are we on our own, alone in the world? Is it somebody you want to be? To me it's interesting to try to figure those things out. Who are you? How do you do it all? How do you do half of it and still make yourself into a person you'd want to know, someone that you could be proud of? How do you stay true to yourself and still give to others? Those are interesting problems to me.

*Do you think you're always going to write screenplays with women at the center of them?*
I don't know. On the one hand, maybe. On the other hand, I kind of hope it's not my undoing. I guarantee you that I will write something with no women in it at all someday, just for the sheer challenge of it. But I love the women I write. But I also love the men. I think I can write a bad guy as good as anybody. I think I can write a misunderstood guy or a Lothario . . .

*That's what I loved about* Something to Talk About. *In that movie you really let the character of Eddie have his say.*
But see, I believe in that. I was as in touch with him as I was with Grace. Maybe more. That's the other thing that pisses me off about the charge of my being unfair to men. If they really think that, then they're not listening. When you read the script you'll see that in *Thelma & Louise,* the male characters were portrayed in a way that was more caricatured on the screen than on the page. And that was a decision made by the male director and the male actors who played them. But that notwithstanding, there are plenty of truck drivers out there who make obscene gestures to women. There is not one single gesture in that script that I didn't witness with my own eyes.

*You didn't design those mudflaps.*

Right. I saw a bumper sticker that read: LICK YOU ALL OVER: TEN CENTS. I saw one of those things that goes around a license plate on the back of a plumbing van that read: SEX INSTRUCTOR; FIRST LESSON FREE. Did that guy think that was gonna help drum up business? These things exist. So the point is there was a reality to those characters whether people like it or not.

*Did you find yourself paying more attention to the male characters when you were writing* Something to Talk About *after the criticism you endured from* Thelma & Louise*?*

No, I didn't. First of all, I paid a lot of attention to the character of Hal, and that just didn't end up in the movie. He had a wife and family, and you saw him really trying to figure out who Thelma and Louise were and what they were going through. Jimmy was a wonderful guy who was just unable to make a commitment at that particular time, but when he realized Louise was going away, he came through. He was there for her. Darryl was a dick, but there are plenty of guys out there who are like that. All you have to do is look at the statistics of spousal abuse to know he's hardly the worst-case scenario. If anything, he's just your average run-of-the-mill dipshit that a lot of women are out there dealing with. But hey, there were people who were upset with the movie because they said it promotes drunk driving, for crying out loud. The kind of criticism that it generated on a certain level was just completely out of proportion with the actual content of the movie. It did demonstrate how hostile people are to women doing anything outside of playing sex objects, sex victims, corpses, or good girls. The description of what women should be in movies was so narrow at the time I wrote that movie that I just couldn't believe it.

*You just blew it all out of the water.*

I just said, "Hey, it doesn't have to be like that." Besides, it's a myth that men didn't like *Thelma & Louise.* I'd be a millionaire if I had a nickel for every time a guy came over and said, "I was one of the few guys that loved that movie." Thousands of men love that movie. And frankly, I think that men are just as bored seeing the same old stupid women characters as women are. I'm not the kind of person that loves a so-called woman's film, where everybody's weepy and profound. It's just not my kind of movie.

*Do you ever start writing with a particular actor in mind?*
Well, I did in this one case with Dennis Quaid. For some reason, when the character of Eddie showed up, he just had his face, his body, his rhythm, everything. And I just prayed like hell that he would get the part. And he did.

*Is he a friend of yours?*
He is now, but I didn't know him when I was writing the part.

*Why did you have his voice in your head?*
That' s just how the character showed up. The Grace in my mind bears no resemblance to Julia Roberts. Thelma and Louise in my mind do not look anything like Geena Davis and Susan Sarandon. It's just a weird thing to have people living in your head.

*Do you see your scripts play out in your head as a movie?*
Oh yeah. Totally. And I know that's never going to see the light of day. It's going to be reinterpreted by hundreds of people on the way to becoming actual. There's only one or two scenes in *Thelma & Louise* that are exactly as I imagined them. One is when Thelma says, "Something's crossed over in me and I can't go back." That scene. The way she says the line, the look on her face, everything, is just so perfect, I can barely watch it. It's just too weird. The other is the holdup scene. I mean, Geena just became Thelma to the point where she couldn't make a mistake. I believe that somehow whatever came to me when I was writing the character then went to her when she was playing it. And I just felt like, "Let her say whatever she wants. Whatever she says is going to be right. She can't make a mistake, 'cause she's fucking channeling now."

*When you're on the set waiting for an actor to say a line you wrote, do you ever fear that they're going to make something else up and you're going to hate it?*

Oh yeah. That happens. You just sit there and seethe quietly. But eventually, you get there. But of course there are times when you think, "Did they read the script? How could they possibly get that reading out of that line?" That's why they talk about its being a painful process for the writer. You cannot just say to an actor, "Come on over here and let me hook you up." And hook your cable into their pack. And they start talking in the character's voice. It's impossible. Although Kyra Sedgwick managed to do it. She just got it.

*She had most of the great lines in the movie. Did you get any complaints from the other actors?*
No, they didn't mention it. I tried to spread the good lines around. But that was just a function of that character. I mean Emma Rae was me just standing there going, "What the fuck are you doing, Grace?" Emma Rae was how I loved Grace in spite of the fact that she frustrated the hell out of me. Kyra said, "I'm just going to play you." I said, "Right. You got it." She was fantastic though and a joy to work with. I can't wait to do it again. I think she's unbelievably talented.

*Why did her character not have more of a life?*
She does. That was just a function of not having more time. Emma Rae ran the auctioneering and real estate part of the business that there was never time to deal with. There's a whole other thing going on that we couldn't deal with. Wyly's an auctioneer. That place is going to be Emma Rae's someday. She was just so connected to it. We just didn't have time for all that in the movie. I probably should have written it as a novel.

*Do you dream about your characters while you're writing them?*
Yes. I walk around thinking about them all the time. While you're writing, it's kind of like being pregnant, and then afterwards, it's a whole other thing with its own life. But I don't spend hours having long conversations with them or anything like that.

*Was Grace a different side of you?*
I think in some ways she was. But I think they all are. People always ask me, "Which are you, Thelma or Louise?" and I think the answer

is both. I totally related to Eddie. When Eddie has that speech where he says, essentially, "I'm a decent guy . . ." I know just how he felt. I think I could be Wyly King if I was a guy and could get away with it. I don't know why, but I never have a character that I can't feel exactly what they're feeling. In a very nonjudgmental way, I can understand why they do what they do, even if I think it's wrong. That's the wonderful thing about writing as opposed to acting. You get to be everybody, only you don't have to do it in front of anyone.

*Do you think that there are two kinds of screenwriters, people with integrity, and people without?*
It's probably not that cut-and-dried. I think that there may be writers who just want to hammer it out and say, "Okay, that's good enough. That'll work. Now go make it and don't bother me." And there're other people who open a vein and bleed all over the page. And unfortunately, I'm more in the latter category. Even if it's not important to anybody else. It's important to me. And I don't really expect it to be as important to anybody else. But it's my job to care more. If I don't, who's going to? The director is going to care more than the writer? I don't think so. At some point a story has to have somebody committed to it more than anything in the world. Like a baby. After a while, they can handle the world, but right at the beginning, somebody's got to be willing to give it everything. A story is like that.

# Thelma & Louise

# Cast

| | |
|---|---|
| Louise | Susan Sarandon |
| Thelma | Geena Davis |
| Hal | Harvey Keitel |
| Jimmy | Michael Madsen |
| Darryl | Christopher McDonald |
| Max | Stephen Tobolowsky |
| J.D. | Brad Pitt |
| Harlan | Timothy Carhart |
| Lena (waitress) | Lucinda Jenney |
| State Trooper | Jason Begh |
| Truck Driver | Marco St. John |

# Filmmakers

| | |
|---|---|
| Writer | Callie Khouri |
| Director | Ridley Scott |
| Producer | Ridley Scott |
| Producer | Mimi Polk |
| Co-Producer | Callie Khouri |
| Co-Producer | Dean O'Brien |
| Director of Photography | Adrian Biddle, B.S.C. |
| Editor | Thom Noble |
| Production Designer | Norris Spencer |
| Music | Hans Zimmer |
| Casting | Louis Di Giaimo, C.S.A. |

LITTLE ROCK, ARKANSAS—PRESENT DAY

INTERIOR. RESTAURANT—MORNING

LOUISE *is a waitress in a coffee shop. She is in her early thirties, but too old to be doing this. She is very pretty and meticulously groomed, even at the end of her shift. She is slamming dirty coffee cups from the counter into a bus tray underneath the counter. It is making a lot of racket which she is oblivious to. There is country Muzak in the background, which she hums along with.*

INT. THELMA'S KITCHEN—MORNING

THELMA *is a housewife. It's morning and she is slamming coffee cups from the breakfast table into the kitchen sink, which is full of dirty breakfast dishes and some stuff left from last night's dinner that had to "soak." She is still in her nightgown. The TV is on in the background. From the kitchen we can see an incomplete wall-papering project going on in the dining room, an obvious do-it-yourself attempt by* THELMA.

INT. RESTAURANT—MORNING

LOUISE *goes to the pay phone and dials a number.*

INT. THELMA'S KITCHEN—MORNING

*Phone rings.* THELMA *goes over to answer it.*

> THELMA
> (*hollering*)

I GOT IT! Hello.

INT. RESTAURANT—MORNING

> LOUISE
> (*at pay phone*)

I hope you're packed, little sister, 'cause we are outta here tonight.

INT. THELMA'S KITCHEN—MORNING

> THELMA
> (*whispering guiltily*)

Well, wait now. I still have to ask Darryl if I can go.

> LOUISE
> (*offscreen, on phone*)

You mean you haven't asked him yet? For christ sake, Thelma, is he your husband or your father? It's just two days. For god's sake, Thelma. Don't be a child. Just tell him you're goin' with me for cryin' out loud. Tell him I'm havin' a nervous breakdown.

THELMA has the phone tucked under her chin as she cuts out coupons from the newspaper and pins them on a bulletin board already covered with them. We see various recipes torn out from women's magazines along the lines of "101 Ways to Cook Pork."

> THELMA

He already thinks you're out of your mind, Louise, that don't carry much weight with Darryl. Are you at work?

> LOUISE
>
> (*offscreen*)

No, I'm callin' from the Playboy Mansion.

THELMA

I'll call you right back.

THELMA goes through the living room to the bottom of the stairs and leans on the banister.

THELMA
(*hollering again*)

Darryl! Honey, you'd better hurry up.

DARRYL comes trotting down the stairs. Polyester was made for this man and he's dripping in "men's" jewelry. He manages a Carpeteria.

DARRYL
(*annoyed*)

Damnit, Thelma, don't holler like that! Haven't I told you I can't stand it when you holler in the morning.

THELMA
(*sweetly and coyly*)

I'm sorry, doll, I just didn't want you to be late.

DARRYL is checking himself out in the hall mirror and it's obvious he likes what he sees. He exudes overconfidence for reasons that never become apparent. He likes to think of himself as a real lady-killer. He is making imperceptible adjustments to his overmoussed hair. THELMA watches approvingly.

THELMA

Hon.

DARRYL
(*still annoyed*)

What.

THELMA
(*She decides not to tell him.*)

Have a good day at work today.

DARRYL

Uh-huh.

THELMA

Hon?

DARRYL

(*as if he's trying to concentrate*)

What?!

THELMA

You want anything special for dinner?

DARRYL

No Thelma, I don't give a shit what we have for dinner. I may not even make it home for dinner. You know how Fridays are.

THELMA

Funny how so many people wanna buy carpet on a Friday night. You'd almost think they'd want to forget about it for the weekend.

DARRYL

Well then, it's a good thing you're not regional manager and I am.

He's finally ready. He walks to the door and gives THELMA the most perfunctory kiss on the cheek.

THELMA

Bye honey. I won't wait up.

DARRYL

Seeya.

DARRYL leaves, and as he closes the front door THELMA leans against it.

THELMA

He's gonna shit.

She goes back into the kitchen and picks up the phone and dials it.

INT. RESTAURANT—MORNING

*The pay phone on the wall rings.* ALBERT, *a busboy in his fifties, answers.*

ALBERT
(*cheerfully*)

Good morning. Why, yes, she is. Is this Thelma? Oh, Thelma, when you gonna run away with me?

LOUISE comes over and takes the phone out of his hand.

LOUISE
(*to* ALBERT)

Not this weekend, sweetie, she's runnin' away with me.
(*Into phone.*) Hi. What'd he say?

Intercut between THELMA and LOUISE.

THELMA

What time are you gonna pick me up?

LOUISE

You're kiddin'! All right! I'll be there around two or three.

THELMA

What kind of stuff do I bring?

LOUISE

I don't know. Warm stuff, I guess. It's the mountains. I guess it gets cold at night. I'm just gonna bring everything.

THELMA

O.K. I will too.

LOUISE

And steal Darryl's fishin' stuff.

THELMA

I don't know how to fish, Louise.

LOUISE

Neither do I , Thelma, but Darryl does it, how hard can it be? I'll see you later. Be ready.

They both hang up.

INT. THELMA'S BEDROOM—DAY

CLOSE-UP *of suitcase on bed. Going into the suitcase are bathing suits, wool socks, flannel pajamas, jeans, sweaters, T-shirts, a couple of dresses, way too much stuff for a two-day trip. Reveal* THELMA, *standing in front of a closet, trying to decide what else to bring, as if she's forgotten something. The room looks like it was decorated entirely from a Sears catalogue. It's really frilly.*

INT. LOUISE'S BEDROOM—DAY

CLOSE-UP *of suitcase on bed. A perfectly ordered suitcase, everything neatly folded and orderly. Three pairs of underwear, one pair of long underwear, two pairs of pants, two sweaters, one furry robe, one nightgown. She could be packing for camp. Reveal* LOUISE. *Her room is as orderly as the suitcase. Everything matches. It's not quite as frilly as* THELMA's, *but it is of the same ilk. She is debating whether to take an extra pair of socks. She decides not to and closes the suitcase. She goes to the phone, picks it up and dials. We hear:*

ANSWERING MACHINE

Hi. This is Jimmy. I'm not here right now but I'll probably be back 'cause . . . all my stuff's here. Leave a message.

LOUISE slams down the phone. A framed picture of LOUISE and JIMMY sits on the table next to the phone. She matter-of-factly slams that facedown too.

INT. THELMA'S BEDROOM—DAY

THELMA *is still throwing stuff in, randomly now. She talks to herself quietly the whole time. She is taking stuff off her nightstand: a small clock, fingernail scissors, etc. She opens the drawer of her nightstand. Her attitude is purpose-*

*ful; she looks as if she knows exactly what she's doing, although frankly, she has no idea, and each decision is completely arbitrary. As she rifles through it, plucking various items from among the jumbled contents, we see there is a gun in there, one* DARRYL *bought her for protection. It is unloaded, but there is a box of bullets. She picks up the gun like it's a rat by the tail and puts it in her purse.*

THELMA
(*muttering to herself*)

Psycho killers . . .

She grabs the box of bullets and throws them in too. She tries to close her suitcase but there is stuff hanging out all over the place. She stuffs things back in the sides and heaves all her weight against the top.

EXT. THELMA'S HOUSE—DAY

*A red '66 Impala convertible in mint condition pulls into the driveway of* THELMA*'s house. The garage door goes up and* THELMA *is standing in the garage with all her gear. A suitcase that looks like it might explode, fishing gear, a cooler, a lantern.* THELMA*'s car, a beat-up gray Honda, is parked in there too.* LOUISE *gets out of the driver's seat.*

LOUISE

We don't need the lantern. The place has electricity.

THELMA
(*pensive*)

I wanna take it anyway. Just in case.

LOUISE

In case of what?

THELMA
(*rationally*)

In case there's some escaped psycho killer on the
loose, who cuts the electricity off and tries to come in
and kill us.

LOUISE
(*going along with her*)

Oh yeah, sure Thelma, that lantern will be real handy.
Maybe we could tow your car behind in case he steals
our spark plugs.

THELMA

We'd have to. That thing barely makes it down the
driveway.

They load everything into the car. The trunk barely closes. THELMA heaves
all her weight against it. They get into the car and pull out of the driveway. As they drive down the street we hear THELMA let out a long howl.
She is laughing and she sticks her arms straight up in the air.

EXT. CAR—DAY

They are driving down the interstate. THELMA reaches for her purse
and finds the gun.

THELMA

Louise, will you take care of the gun?

LOUISE shrieks at the sight of it.

LOUISE
(*startled*)

Why in hell did you bring that?

THELMA wonders if LOUISE is really that naive.

THELMA

Oh come on Louise ... psycho killers, bears ... snakes! I just don't know how to use it. So will you take care of it?

LOUISE reaches over and takes the gun out of THELMA's purse and holds it in her hand. She tests the weight of it and then puts it under the seat. THELMA puts the bullets under the seat.

THELMA

I'm just really afraid of psycho killers, I guess.

They are speeding off down the highway with the radio blaring. LOUISE puts in a tape of wild R&B music.

THELMA

Whose place is this again?

LOUISE

It's Bob's, the day manager's. He's gettin' a divorce, so his wife's gettin' this place, so he's just lettin' all his friends use it till he has to turn over the keys.

THELMA

I've never been out of town without Darryl.

LOUISE

How come he let you go?

THELMA

'Cause I didn't ask him.

LOUISE

Aw shit, Thelma, he's gonna kill you.

THELMA

Well, he'd have never let me go. He never lets me do one goddamn thing that's any fun. All he wants me to do is hang around the house the whole time while he's out doing God only knows what.

They are both silent for a minute.

THELMA
(*looking straight ahead*)

I left him a note. I left him stuff to microwave.

After a pause:

THELMA
(*carefully*)

I guess you haven't heard anything from Jimmy . . . yet?

LOUISE's jaw tightens. The car speeds up.

THELMA

. . . nevermind.

A huge semi-trailer passes them on the highway and honks.

THELMA
(*smiling*)

One of your friends?


**LATER**

INT. CAR—DAY

DRIVING SHOT. THELMA *is watching herself in the side mirror, pretending to smoke a cigarette.*

THELMA'S POINT OF VIEW*: a sign alongside the road that reads* SEE YOU IN CHURCH ON SUNDAY!

THELMA *pushes in the lighter and waits for it to pop out.* LOUISE *gives her a sidelong glance but does not say anything.*

INT. CAR—COUNTRY ROAD—DAY

THELMA

How much longer is it gonna be? I'm starving.

LOUISE

Just another hour or so. We'll eat when we get to the cabin. We've got enough food for a month . . .

THELMA

Can't we just stop for a few minutes . . . I'll never make it . . .

LOUISE

We're not gonna get to the cabin till after dark as it is . . .

THELMA
(*whining*)

Then what difference does it make if we stop? Come
on. I never get to do stuff like this.

LOUISE realizes that THELMA is going to revert to a teenager and continue whining unless she gives in.

LOUISE

All right, but it's gonna be quick.

They drive down the road until they see a place down on the right all
lit up with neon. It's called the Idle Hour. The sign flashes: COCKTAILS—
BEER—DANCING—FOOD.

There is a huge gravel parking lot with lots of pickup trucks and
older cars. Even though it's early, you can tell this place is a real
nightspot. It's already pretty crowded.

INT. IDLE HOUR—NIGHT

*This place is jumpin'. There are ten pool tables with crowds all around. The
long bar is filled with customers. There are tables and booths. The room is
dense with smoke. There is a dance floor, but no one is dancing yet because
the band is still setting up. There are a lot of single men. Many heads turn
and follow* THELMA *and* LOUISE *to an empty table.*

LOUISE

I haven't seen a place like this since I left Texas.

THELMA

Idn't this fun?

A waitress, LENA, comes over and drops two menus on the table.

LENA

Y'all wanna drink?

LOUISE

No thanks.

THELMA

I'd like a Wild Turkey straight up and a Coke back, please.

As LENA leaves:

LOUISE
(*surprised*)

Thelma!

THELMA
(*annoyed*)

Tell me somethin'. Is this my vacation or isn't it. I mean God, you're as bad as Darryl.

LOUISE

I just haven't seen you like this in a while. I'm used to seeing you more sedate.

THELMA

Well, I've had it up to my ass with sedate! You said you and me was gonna get outta town and for once just really let our hair down. Well, darlin', look out 'cause my hair is comin' down!

As LENA returns:

> LOUISE
> (*laughing*)

All right. (*To* LENA:) I changed my mind. I'll have a margarita with a shot of Cuervo on the side, please.

> THELMA

Yeah!

As LENA leaves, a MAN comes over with a chair, which he pulls up to the table and straddles backward. He is in his late forties, heavyset, and his face is shiny in the neon light.

> MAN

Now what are a couple of kewpie dolls like you doin' in a place like this?

| LOUISE | THELMA |
|---|---|
| (*coldly*) | (*real friendly*) |
| Mindin' our own business, why don't you try it. | Well, we left town for the weekend 'cause we wanted to try and have a good time. And because Louise here is mad because her boyfriend won't call her while he's out on the road . . . |

LOUISE kicks THELMA under the table.

> THELMA
> (*quieter*)

We just wanted to get somethin' to eat.

MAN

Well, you come to the right place. You like chili? They
got good chili.

LENA returns with LOUISE's drinks.

WAITRESS

Harlan, are you botherin' these poor girls?

HARLAN

Hell no. I'm just bein' friendly.

LENA
(*making eye contact with* LOUISE)

It's a good thing they're not all as friendly as you.

LOUISE understands.

THELMA

Your name's Harlan? I got an uncle named Harlan!

HARLAN

You do? Is he a funny uncle? 'Cause if he is then he
and I got somethin' in common.

HARLAN laughs. THELMA laughs too, but doesn't really get the joke.
LOUISE does not laugh.

LOUISE
(*to* HARLAN)

I don't mean to be rude, but I've got something I need

to talk to my friend about. In private. And this is the
first chance we've had . . .

HARLAN

Aw, I understand. I didn't mean to bother ya. It's just
hard not to notice two such pretty ladies as yourself.
(*Standing, to* THELMA:) You better dance with me before you leave, or I'll never forgive ya.

THELMA
( *friendly*)

Oh, sure. That'd be fun.

HARLAN leaves, then:

THELMA

Jeez Louise, that wasn't very nice.

LOUISE

God, you're naive. Can't you tell when somebody's
hittin' on you?

THELMA

So what if he was? Nothin' was gonna happen. I'm not
naive. It's just all your years of waitin' tables has made
you jaded, that's all.

LOUISE

Maybe. I just didn't like the way he was lookin' at you.
He was makin' me nervous.

THELMA

Well, just relax, will ya. You're makin' me nervous.

THELMA knocks back her shot of Wild Turkey and holds up her glass to LENA to bring her another one. LENA sees her and nods. She turns back to face her friend.

THELMA

So, Jimmy still hasn't called yet?

LOUISE
(*trying not to seem upset*)

Givin' him a taste of his own medicine. See how he likes it. (*Now she's upset.*) Asshole.

THELMA
(*sympathetically*)

I'm sorry Louise. I know you're all upset and here I am not even thinkin' about you. It's just I'm so excited to be out of the house, I guess. (*Pause.*) I wonder if Darryl's home yet.

LOUISE
(*wistful*)

I wonder if Jimmy's gotten back.

THELMA

Why don't you tell him to just get lost, once and for all?

LOUISE

Why don't you ditch that loser husband of yours?

They both drift off momentarily, contemplating their domestic problems, until LENA comes over.

> LENA
> (*rolling her eyes*)

This one's on Harlan.

THELMA looks over at the bar where HARLAN is grinning at her, making dancing motions. She smiles and waves at him. Her face becomes serious again as she turns back to LOUISE.

> THELMA

> Well, look. Don't be such a gloomy gus. Jimmy'll come in off the road, you won't be there, he'll freak out and call you a hundred thousand times and Sunday night, you'll call him back and by Monday everything will be back to normal.

THELMA's mind goes too fast for her mouth and the speed at which she speaks can be staggering. LOUISE is used to it. LOUISE smiles wistfully at THELMA's assessment of the situation.

> LOUISE
> (*looking dejected*)

Yeah, I guess.

> THELMA

> In the meantime you said we were gonna have some fun. So let's have some!

She again drinks her whole shot of Wild Turkey and holds up her glass as the band strikes up a lively tune. Practically the whole place "whoops" and heads for the dance floor. LOUISE drinks her shot of tequila and holds up her glass too.

**LATER**

THELMA is dancing with HARLAN and has been for quite a while. LOUISE has been dancing with a quiet guy named Dan. THELMA is breathless, drunk and giggly. She holds a beer bottle in one hand. She is laughing a lot about nothing and HARLAN is studying her closely. LOUISE notices this.

> LOUISE
> (*over the noise*)

Thelma, I'm gonna hit the little girls room and then we gotta hit the road.

> THELMA
> (*eyes closed, swaying with the music*)

Ready when you are.

LOUISE heads off to the bathroom.

> THELMA
> (*eyes still closed*)

Louise, I'm gonna come with you.

She gets a funny look on her face.

> THELMA

I don't feel so good.

She stumbles a step and drops her beer bottle.

CUT TO: LOUISE heading toward the bathroom, where there is a line of at least fifteen women in front of her. CUT TO:

> HARLAN
> (*catching* THELMA, *copping feels*)

Oopsy doopsy. We need to get you some fresh air, little lady.

He steers her toward the door.

CUT TO: LOUISE leaning against the wall, waiting in line.

EXT. PARKING LOT—NIGHT

HARLAN *is hauling* THELMA *out the door into the parking lot. She is pretty limp.*

                    THELMA

Oh shit.

                    HARLAN

What's wrong?

                    THELMA

Stop.

                    HARLAN

What for?

                    THELMA

I'm spinning.

INT. IDLE HOUR—NIGHT

LENA *is going over to their table. She picks up* THELMA*'s purse off the floor and puts it on her chair. She sets the check on the table, looks around to see if she can see them and walks away.*

INT. BATHROOM—NIGHT

LOUISE *goes into the bathroom. She stands in front of the sink and looks at herself in the mirror.*

EXT. PARKING LOT—NIGHT

THELMA *has been sick. She has* HARLAN *'s handkerchief and is wiping her mouth.* HARLAN *has backed off for this part but he's right back in there.*

> HARLAN
>
> How you feelin' now, darlin?

HARLAN is leaning close to THELMA's head and she pulls her head away.

> THELMA
>
> I guess I'm startin' to feel a little better.

> HARLAN
>
> Yeah, you're startin' to feel pretty good to me too.

He pulls her to him and tries to put his arms around her. THELMA pulls away.

> THELMA
> (*uncomfortable*)
>
> I think I need to keep walking.

INT. IDLE HOUR—NIGHT

LOUISE comes out of the bathroom as the next woman goes in. She scans the room looking for THELMA. She doesn't see her. She goes over to the table and sees THELMA's stuff there. She picks up the check and looks at it.

EXT. PARKING LOT—NIGHT

HARLAN *has led* THELMA *off to the far end of the parking lot. He is trying to kiss her now. She is pushing his arms down and turning her head away.*

THELMA

Don't. I'm married. I don't feel good. I've been sick.

HARLAN

It's O.K. I'm married too.

HARLAN is pushing himself on her now and she is beginning to push him away harder.

INT. IDLE HOUR—NIGHT

LOUISE *is paying* LENA. LENA *is shaking her head indicating she hasn't seen* THELMA *either.* LOUISE *picks up* THELMA*'s stuff and heads toward the door.*

EXT. PARKING LOT—NIGHT

HARLAN *has now pinned* THELMA *against the back of a car and is kissing her neck. He has her ass in his hands. He is beginning to hump her. She is pushing him away as hard as she can but he is relentless.*

HARLAN
(*breathing heavily*)

You're beautiful. It's O.K. I won't hurt you. It's O.K.

THELMA
(*struggling*)

Stop it! Goddamnit, I mean it! Louise is gonna wonder where I am. Let go!

HARLAN

Louise is all right.

CUT TO: LOUISE is now standing outside the door of the Idle Hour. She is looking around. CUT TO: HARLAN is pulling at THELMA's clothes. THELMA gets one of her arms free and hits him hard in the face. He hits her back and grabs her face, squeezing it hard.

> HARLAN

Don't you hit me! Don't you fucking hit me!

There is no trace of friendliness in his face now. He looks mean and dangerous. He lets go of her face and pins her arms behind her. He holds both of her arms with one hand.

> HARLAN

You just shut up.

With his free hand he reaches down and starts to pull her dress up. THELMA is still struggling and there are tears running down her face.

> THELMA
> (*reasoning with him*)

Don't hurt me. Harlan. Please.

> HARLAN
> (*mean*)

Shut up.

He turns her around, pushing her facedown onto the back of the car. He holds both her arms in one hand and continues pulling her dress up over her hips. He starts to undo his pants as we hear the crunch of gravel.

> LOUISE
> (*calmly*)

Let her go.

>                         HARLAN
>                         (*mean*)
>
> Get lost.
>
>                         THELMA
>
> Louise!

TIGHT SHOT of the barrel of THELMA's gun being pressed into the nape of HARLAN's neck. LOUISE's thumb pulls back the hammer.

>                         LOUISE
>                         (*calmly*)
>
> Let her go, you fucking asshole, or I'm going to splat-
> ter your ugly face all over this nice car.

HARLAN slowly raises his hands in the air and THELMA darts out, pulling her dress down.

>                         HARLAN
>                         (*scared*)
>
> Now, calm down. We were just havin' a little fun.

LOUISE glances at THELMA. THELMA shakes her head no.

>                         LOUISE
>
> Looks like you've got a real fucked-up idea of fun. Now
> turn around.

LOUISE starts to back away but the gun is still close to his face. His pants are undone in the front. She is still backing away with the gun raised. THELMA is inching away as well.

>                         LOUISE
>
> Just for the future, when a woman's crying like that,
> she's not having any fun.

LOUISE lowers the gun and stares at him for a second. Then she turns and walks away. THELMA does too.

> HARLAN
> (*angry, pulling up his pants*)

Bitch. I should have gone ahead and fucked her.

LOUISE stops in her tracks.

> LOUISE

What did you say?

> HARLAN
> (*smiling, arrogant*)

I said suck my cock.

LOUISE takes two long strides back toward him, raises the gun and fires a bullet into his face. We hear his body hit the gravel parking lot.
     LOUISE'S POINT OF VIEW: the car behind him is splattered with blood. THELMA and LOUISE are both silent. We hear the sound of the nightclub in the distance. LOUISE lowers the gun.

> THELMA
> (*stunned*)

Oh my God.

> LOUISE
> (*still calm, emotionless*)

Get the car.

> THELMA

Jesus Christ, Louise, you shot him.

> LOUISE

Get the car!

THELMA runs to get the car.

> LOUISE
> (*quietly to herself*)

You watch your mouth, buddy.

THELMA comes careening up in reverse. LOUISE hops in and THELMA peels out, spraying gravel. As they speed out of the parking lot back to the road, we hear music blaring from the nightclub. They hit the main road with tires squealing.

> LOUISE

Get back to the interstate.

LOUISE lifts her hand and notices she is still holding the gun.

> THELMA
> (*panicked, trying to stay calm*)

Shit! I . . . I, which way?

> LOUISE
> (*dazed*)

West. Left.

EXT. CAR—NIGHT

DISTANCING SHOT. *They get onto the interstate going west.*

INT. CAR—NIGHT

LOUISE *picks up the handkerchief from the car seat and wipes the gun off. Her movements are as if in slow motion. She puts the gun under the seat.* THELMA *is watching her.*

> THELMA
> (*carefully*)

Louise.

LOUISE does not answer.

> THELMA

Louise. Where are we going?

> LOUISE
> (*shaking*)

I don't know, Thelma! I don't know! Just shut up a minute so I can think.

THELMA starts to cry quietly.

> LOUISE
> (*slightly hysterical*)

Oh my God. Oh my God.

> THELMA
> (*trying to think straight*)

Shouldn't we go to the cops? I mean I think we should tell the police.

> LOUISE
> (*snapping*)

Tell them what?! What Thelma? What do you think we should tell them?

> THELMA
> (*crying*)

I don't know. We just tell 'em what happened.

> LOUISE

Which part?

> THELMA

All of it. That he tried to rape me.

LOUISE
(*sharply*)

Only about a hundred people saw you cheek to
goddamn cheek with him all night, Thelma! Who's
gonna believe that?! We just don't live in that kind of
a world.

An animal runs across the road in front of the car and THELMA swerves
to avoid it. The tires squeal.

LOUISE

Pull over!

THELMA pulls off to the side of the road. LOUISE gets out and starts to
walk around the car. She stops when she gets to the back of the car
and she is sick. THELMA waits in the car and moves over to the passenger side. LOUISE gets in the driver's side.

THELMA

Louise . . . Are you all right?

LOUISE rests her head on the steering wheel. Off in the distance there
are sirens.

LOUISE
(*to herself, helplessly*)

Oh Christ.

She puts the car in gear and pulls back onto the interstate.

EXT. TRUCK STOP—4 A.M.

LOUISE *pulls into the huge parking area of a large truck stop. Even at this
time of morning the place is a beehive of activity.* THELMA *stares out her window, not seeing.* LOUISE *stops the car.*

LOUISE

Thelma.

THELMA doesn't hear.

LOUISE

Thelma.

THELMA looks at her blankly, without answering.

LOUISE

I've gotta stop for a minute. I've got to get it together.
I just got to take a break. Now, I'm going in there. I'm
gonna get a cup of coffee and I'm gonna sit down for
a second. Do you want to come?

THELMA's head moves almost imperceptibly. LOUISE studies THELMA's
face.

LOUISE

Is that yes? Are you up to this?

Again THELMA slightly moves her head in a nod.

LOUISE

We gotta be inconspicuous. Do you know what that
means?

THELMA

Yes.

LOUISE

It means you don't talk to anybody. You don't draw attention to yourself in any way. Do you understand that?

Again she twitches more than nods.

LOUISE

Tell me you understand that.

THELMA nods more firmly now. She understands.
    Various POINT OF VIEW shots of truck drivers seeing THELMA and LOUISE wind their way toward the restaurant portion of the coffee shop. They look small and incongruous against the surroundings.

INT. TRUCK STOP—4 A.M.

TIGHT SHOT *of a waitress's hands slamming dirty coffee cups from the counter into a bus tray underneath the counter. Reveal* LOUISE *and* THELMA *sitting at the counter.* LOUISE *is looking at a map.* THELMA *is in a daze. The car is parked outside, near the door.*

LOUISE
(*halfway to herself*)

We have to think this through. We have to be smart. Now is not the time to panic. If we panic now, we're done for. Nobody saw it. Nobody knows it was us. We're still O.K. Now all we have to do is just figure out our next move.

THELMA
(*sarcastically*)

Our next move? I'll say one thing, Louise. This is some vacation. I sure am having a good time. This is really fun.

LOUISE
(*sharply*)

If you weren't so concerned with having a good time
we wouldn't be here right now.

THELMA

Just what is that supposed to mean?

LOUISE

It means shut up, Thelma.

THELMA

So this is my fault, is it?

LOUISE looks at THELMA for a long time.

LOUISE

Just shut up.

The waitress comes and fills their coffee cups.

EXT. IDLE HOUR PARKING LOT—4 A.M.

*Police cars are parked all around. The activity has died down. Doors on the
coroner's van slam shut. In the back of a police car sits* LENA *with the door
open. A detective,* HAL, *in a suit leans over the car door with his notepad.*

HAL

Could you identify 'em if ya saw 'em again?

LENA

Hal, I've told you about twenty times, yes I could identify 'em, but neither one of them was the type to pull something like this.

HAL

Well, you're not exactly an expert witness, but what makes you so sure?

LENA

If waitin' tables in a bar don't make you an expert on human nature, then nothin' will, and I could've told you that Harlan Puckett would end up buyin' it in a parkin' lot. I'm just surprised it didn't happen before now.

HAL

Who do you think did it?

LENA

Has anybody asked his wife? She's the one I hope did it.

HAL

Lena, just cut the bullshit, will ya? Do ya have any ideas or don't ya? I been standin' in this stupid parkin' lot all goddamn night and I still got to go file a report before I can go home in time to get back up again!

LENA

Well, if I had to guess, I'd say it was either some ol' gal, or some ol' gal's husband. But it wasn't either one of those two. The smaller one, the one with the tidy hairdo. She left a huge tip.

HAL

You didn't happen to notice what kind of car they were driving?

LENA

It's a nightclub, not a drive-in, Hal. I don't follow the customers to the parking lot.

HAL

All right Lena. Go on home. We might have to call you in for some more questioning.

LENA gets out of the back of the car.

LENA

Those girls was not the murderous type.

INT. TRUCK STOP—NIGHT

THELMA

I have to go to the bathroom.

THELMA stands up to go to the bathroom. She grabs her purse from the counter and the strap catches on her coffee cup and it falls to the floor with a crash. All heads turn and look at her.

THELMA

I . . . Sorry.

INT. PAY PHONE—NIGHT

*Outside the bathroom there is a pay phone.* THELMA *picks it up and dials.*

> THELMA
> (*into phone*)

Collect from Thelma.

There is no answer.

INT. THELMA'S HOUSE—NIGHT

*Phone rings.*

VARIOUS SHOTS of the interior of the empty Dickinson house:

> The bedroom exactly as THELMA left it.
> The drawer of the nightstand still open.
> The note to Darryl taped to the refrigerator.
> The interior of the microwave with a now completely thawed microwave dinner still in the package in a little puddle.

INT. TRUCK STOP—NIGHT

> THELMA

Thanks. I'll try later.

She hangs up and goes into the bathroom. As the door closes behind her, LOUISE comes up with a handful of change and starts putting it into the phone. She dials a number. It rings for a long time. She hangs up and goes into the bathroom. She looks at herself in the mirror. She notices a tiny speck on her cheek. She takes a paper towel and wets it and rubs the spot. She looks at the towel and there is a bright red streak.

LOUISE
(*urgently*)

Come on Thelma!

The door of the stall flies open and THELMA comes charging out and heads straight for the door without even looking at LOUISE. LOUISE charges out after her. They head out of the restaurant, and through the window we see them get into the car and drive away.

EXT. CAR—DAWN

DRIVING SHOT. *The top is down on the car, and* THELMA *is slouched on the seat, her hair blowing wildly.* LOUISE *is wearing a scarf, and the hair that shows barely moves.*

LOUISE
(*thinking out loud, mechanical*)

We're gonna go to the next town and stop. We'll get a motel room. I can rest for a while and then figure out how to get some money. We're gonna need money. Thelma. How much money do you have with you?

THELMA

What? Oh, I don't know. Let me look.

Off in the distance, there is a person standing on the side of the road. THELMA is rummaging through her purse. She finds her wallet and takes it out. THELMA finds some bills stuffed in the change compartment and takes them out. She straightens the money out.

THELMA

Sixty-four dollars.

As she is counting it, one of the bills flies out of her hands. THELMA's not that good at handling money.

THELMA

Umm. Shit. Forty-four dollars.

LOUISE has not noticed any of this, as she is so intent on her driving.

THELMA

I'm cash poor. I've got credit cards.

LOUISE

Hmmm. We gotta get some money.

EXT. MOTEL—DAY

ESTABLISHING SHOT. *The motel is in an agricultural area with an interstate nearby.*

INT. MOTEL ROOM—DAY (6 A.M.)

*The curtains are open and we can see the car parked right outside the room.* THELMA *is lying on the bed staring up at the ceiling.* LOUISE *is bustling around the room, putting things in drawers.*

THELMA

Why are you unpacking? You said we were just gonna take a nap.

LOUISE did not realize she was doing it.

LOUISE
(*frustrated*)

Oh, I don't know. I'm just nervous. I gotta figure out what to do.

THELMA

Well, when you figure it out, wake me up.

LOUISE slams the closet door. THELMA jumps.

LOUISE

Just what the hell is wrong with you?

THELMA

What do you mean?

LOUISE

Why are you actin' like this?

THELMA

Actin' like what?! How am I supposed to act? 'Scuse me for not knowing what to do after you blow somebody away!

They are silent for a moment.

LOUISE

You could help me try and figure it out! I gotta figure out what to do and you could TRY and help me.

THELMA

I suggested we go to the police, but you didn't like that, so frankly Louise, I'm all out of ideas.

LOUISE

Well, what's the big rush, Thelma? If we just give 'em
some time, they'll come to us! . . . Oh Christ. Listen, I
. . . I just don't know what to do. Why don't you go
out to the pool or something and I'll figure it out . . .
I'm just not ready to go to jail yet.

THELMA

Give me the keys.

LOUISE

You're not touchin' that car.

THELMA

My stuff's in the trunk! God! You care more about that
car than you do about most people.

LOUISE

Most people just cause me trouble, but that car always
gets me out of it.

INT. POLICE GARAGE—DAY

HAL *is at the police station, where they're dusting the car with* HARLAN *all over
it for prints.* HAL *looks closely at the back of the car. He holds his hands over
two sets of handprints. He moves his hands to the outside of the prints so as
not to smear them. He leans down and is in almost the same position that*
THELMA *was in, his face one inch away from the trunk. He sees a very clear
drop of blood. It's different than any of the other spatters on the car. He calls
the identification technician over and points it out.* HAL *takes a Sharpie and
draws a circle around the drop.*

EXT. MOTEL—DAY

THELMA *comes out of the room and walks toward the pool.* TIGHT SHOT *of* THELMA*'s eyes. She stops, then decides to go on to the pool. She lies down in a lounge chair facing the road.*

INT. MOTEL ROOM—DAY

LOUISE *is in the motel room. She's looking at the phone. She picks it up and dials it and watches herself in the mirror. She stares as if she's trying to see into herself, see through herself.*

EXT. MOTEL POOL—DAY

THELMA *arranges herself in a lounge chair, trying desperately to feel like she's on vacation.*

INT. MOTEL ROOM—DAY

ANSWERING MACHINE

Hi. This is Jimmy. I'm not here right now . . .

A voice interrupts the message.

JIMMY
(*offscreen, on phone*)

Hello! I'm here. Hang on a minute!

The machine switches off.

INT. JIMMY'S APARTMENT—DAY

JIMMY, *mid-thirties, musician, is standing in the kitchen on the phone. He's not the type you'd expect* LOUISE *to like, not quite straight looking enough.*

LOUISE
(*offscreen, on phone*)

Jimmy . . .

INT. MOTEL ROOM—DAY

LOUISE *is looking at herself on the phone in the mirror. She is very choked up.*

JIMMY
(*offscreen, on phone*)

Louise! Where are you? Are you all right? Honey . . .

LOUISE
(*regaining composure*)

Hi. I'm O.K. How are you? Long time, no see.

JIMMY
(*offscreen, concerned*)

Louise, honey . . . Where are you? You sound funny.

LOUISE *is still looking at herself in the mirror, as if she's never seen herself before.*

LOUISE

I am funny. I'm real funny.

JIMMY
(*offscreen*)

Are you in town? This sounds long-distance.

LOUISE

No, I'm out of town. I'm in . . . I'm in real deep shit, Jimmy. Deep shit Arkansas.

                              JIMMY
                    (*offstcreen, now very concerned*)

Louise, just tell me what the hell is going on here! I
come back, nobody knows where you are. Is Thelma
with you? Darryl's been callin' here every half hour
sayin' he's gonna kill you both when you get back, he's
goin' nuts. I don't envy her if she is.

EXT. MOTEL POOL—DAY

THELMA *at the pool basking in the sun.*

INT. MOTEL ROOM—DAY

                              JIMMY
                      (*offscreen, on phone*)

Where'd y'all go?

                             LOUISE

Fishing. Look, Jimmy . . . I need you to help me. This
is serious. I'm in trouble and I need you to help me.
Can you do that? (*She is about to cry.*) Jimmy?

INT. JIMMY'S APARTMENT—DAY

JIMMY *is shocked by the gravity of her tone of voice. He realizes this is very serious.*

                              JIMMY

Yes, yes darlin'. I can help you. Tell me where you are.

INT. MOTEL ROOM—DAY

                             LOUISE

Something real bad has happened and I can't tell you

what, just that it's bad and I did it and I can't undo it.
Can you hold on a minute?

LOUISE covers the mouthpiece with her hand. She is trying very hard
not to cry.

> LOUISE

I have a savings account with about sixty-seven hundred dollars in it. Now I know you won't be able to
get it out, but I'm good for it. I need that money. Can
you wire me sixty-seven hundred dollars and I'll pay
you back? Please, I'm desperate.

> JIMMY
> (*offscreen, getting very upset*)

Of course. Of course! Where? Can't I bring it to you?
For god's sake, baby, please, just tell me what's happened, what could possibly be so bad?

LOUISE sits on the edge of the bed. She is looking at her hand.

> LOUISE

Jimmy?

She takes the ring that she wears on her left hand and turns it around
backward to make it look like a wedding band.

> LOUISE

Do you love me?

> JIMMY
> (*offscreen*)

Christ, yes!

LOUISE

How come you never married me?

JIMMY
(*offscreen; desperate, almost hysterical*)

Louise! I . . . I . . . I don't know! What . . . where . . .

LOUISE

Wire it to the Western Union in Oklahoma City.

INT. JIMMY'S APARTMENT—DAY

JIMMY

You're in Oklahoma?!

LOUISE
(*offscreen, on phone*)

Not yet.

JIMMY
(*thinking fast*)

Louise, let me call you back after I wire it so you'll know which office to go to.

LOUISE
(*offscreen*)

Can't it go to any office?

JIMMY

No, for that much money I have to tell them exactly which office. I know, I've had to have money wired to me on the road. And there has to be a code word or they won't give it to you. I'll have to tell you the code.

INT. MOTEL ROOM—DAY

> LOUISE

Tell me now.

> JIMMY
> (*offscreen, on phone*)

Call me back.

> LOUISE

O.K. I'll call you back. In an hour. Don't tell Darryl.

> JIMMY
> (*offscreen*)

I know. Call me back. Louise, I love you, O.K.?

> LOUISE

O.K.

EXT. MOTEL POOL—DAY

THELMA *is by the pool. Her mouth is open. She's asleep. A car screeches, a loud horn honks.*

> LOUISE
> (*bellowing*)

Come on Thelma! Get in the car!

THELMA bolts upright and grabs her sundress and dashes to the car. She jumps in over the door. She's in a mild state of shock.

> THELMA

Did you finish thinking?

LOUISE

I think better when I drive.

LOUISE peels out of the parking lot.

INT. DAY—POLICE STATION

HAL *is in an office talking to his superior. He stands in front of the desk with his hands in his pockets while his* MAJOR *sits behind the desk looking troubled.*

HAL

All we know is there were two women in a red Chevy convertible that turned left out of the parking lot, going real fast. We're trying to get a make on the car, but nothin' yet. So far, we got nothin'.

MAJOR

Well, you'd best get something. Even if they didn't do it, it times out that they most likely witnessed it. I want somebody to at least talk to 'em. Put out an APB with a description and see what comes back.

HAL

All right.

MAJOR

Somebody's butt is gonna bar-be-que.

EXT. CAR—FARMLAND—DAY

DRIVING SHOT.

INT. CAR—DAY

                    THELMA

Don't get mad, Louise, but where are we going?

                    LOUISE

Oklahoma City. Jimmy's gonna wire me some money
and then . . .

                    THELMA

You talked to him?! Is he mad? Did you tell him?

                    LOUISE

No, I didn't tell him. And that's something we gotta
get straight. Darryl was callin', mad as a hornet, makin'
all kinds of noise. When you talk to him, you *cannot*
say anything about this. You gotta make everything
sound normal.

                    THELMA

I called the asshole at four in the morning and he
wasn't even home. I don't know what he's got to be
mad about. I'm the one who should be mad.

                    LOUISE

I've been tellin' you that for the last ten years.

                    THELMA

Do you think Darryl's having an affair?

LOUISE

I don't think Darryl is mature enough to conduct an affair.

THELMA

But you think he fools around.

LOUISE
(*quietly, to* THELMA)

Thelma, I'm going to Mexico. I think I can make it in two and a half days, but I'm going to have to haul ass. Are you up to this? I mean, I have to know. This isn't a game. I'm in deep shit. I gotta know what you're gonna do.

THELMA
(*stunned*)

I . . . I don't know. I don't know what you're askin' me.

LOUISE
(*serious*)

Don't you fall apart on me, goddamnit, Thelma. Every time we get in trouble, you go blank or plead insanity or some such shit and this time . . . Not this time. Everything's changed now . . . Now you can do whatever you want. You can catch a bus, whatever, but I'm going to Mexico. I'm going. Are you coming with me?

THELMA is staring down the road. She does not answer. Then:

THELMA

I think he does. Fool around.

EXT. CAR—DAY

DRIVING SHOT.

INT. DAY—POLICE STATION

TIGHT SHOT *of an "ident-a-kit" likeness of* LOUISE. *On a table nearby lays a drawing strongly resembling* THELMA. LENA, *the waitress, sits next to the plainclothes cop who holds the ident-a-kit.* HAL *picks up the drawing and studies it closely.*

INT. FBI OFFICE—DAY

*Tight shot of a fax machine with the ident-a-kit drawing of* LOUISE *coming out. A* MAN *takes it out, looks at it and walks across the room full of desks and typewriters, computer terminals, etc. On the wall is the symbol of the FBI and* Federal Bureau of Investigation *is spelled out underneath it. The* MAN *walks into an office and hands several sheets of fax paper, including police sketches of* THELMA *and* LOUISE, *to a* MAN *sitting behind a desk. The* MAN *looks questioningly at the man who brought him the papers.*

MAX

I know. They're just wanted for questioning for now.

EXT./INT. COUNTRY STORE—DAY

LOUISE *and* THELMA *pull up in front of an old store, the kind with a wooden front porch, the kind that sells bait and flannel shirts. They enter the store and see an* OLD MAN *behind the counter.*

LOUISE

Do you have a pay phone?

OLD MAN

'Round the side, by the restrooms.

LOUISE gets change while THELMA strolls around, looking at rubber worms and pickled pigs' feet. LOUISE goes out to the phone.

EXT. PAY PHONE—DAY

LOUISE *is dropping change into the phone. It rings and* JIMMY *answers.*

INT. JIMMY'S APARTMENT—DAY

> JIMMY

Louise!

EXT. PAY PHONE—DAY

> LOUISE

Is that how you answer the phone?

> JIMMY
> (*offscreen, on phone*)

I got it. I was afraid I'd missed you. I almost couldn't get a check cashed. It's Saturday.

> LOUISE

Who did it?

> JIMMY
> (*offscreen*)

Friend of mine, owns a club. Dickie Randall. You'd know him if you saw him. His brother was in your class. Terry.

> LOUISE

You didn't say what it was for, did you?

> JIMMY
> (*offscreen*)

No, honey. I told him I was buyin' a car. (*Serious.*) What is it for?

> LOUISE
> (*not responding to the question*)

Good. That was good. Where do I go?

> JIMMY
> (*offscreen*)

It's a place called Shaw's Siesta Motel. The address is 1989 Northeast 23. It's under your name.

> LOUISE

And what's the mysterious code word?

> JIMMY
> (*offscreen*)

Peaches.

> LOUISE

What.

> JIMMY
> (*offscreen*)

That's the code word. I miss you, peaches.

LOUISE rolls her eyes and tries not to melt.

> LOUISE

O.K., Jimmy. Thanks.

She puts her finger down on the receiver.

INT. JIMMY'S APARTMENT—DAY

JIMMY *is still holding the phone to his ear.*

> JIMMY

Louise?

INT. COUNTRY STORE—DAY

THELMA *is in the store buying gum, beef jerky. Next to the cash register on the counter on display are those little tiny bottles of liquor.* THELMA *picks up a little bottle of Wild Turkey and puts it on the counter. The* OLD MAN *rings it up. She takes another one and puts it on the counter. The* OLD MAN *is still ringing stuff up. She takes two more and puts them on the counter. She takes the rest of the little bottles of Wild Turkey out of the display and puts them on the counter. She takes one little bottle of Cuervo and puts that down too. The old man finally looks at her. From the wall behind him he takes a pint of Wild Turkey down.*

> OLD MAN

Ma'am, are you sure you wouldn't rather have the large economy size?

EXT. PAY PHONE—DAY

LOUISE *is hanging up the phone. She walks away, toward the front of the store.*

EXT. COUNTRY STORE—DAY

THELMA *comes out of the front of the store.*

> LOUISE

Go call Darryl.

THELMA is walking toward the car. She puts her purse in the front seat. She looks at LOUISE.

> THELMA
>
> Call him?

> LOUISE
>
> Call him. Don't tell him anything. Tell him you're having a wonderful time and you'll be home tomorrow night.

> THELMA
>
> Will I be?

> LOUISE
>
> I don't know. I won't be.

THELMA and LOUISE look at each other while this sinks in. THELMA walks around to the side of the building to the phone. She picks it up and dials.

> THELMA
>
> Collect from Thelma.

EXT. STOREFRONT—DAY

LOUISE *goes into the store for a chocolate Yoo-Hoo.*

EXT. PAY PHONE—DAY

> THELMA
> (*unsteadily*)
>
> Honey?

INT. THELMA'S HOUSE—DAY

DARRYL *is in the den of their house. The room is a mess. There are beer cans everywhere. The large screen TV is on, showing a football game.* DARRYL *is in a recliner. He is wearing loud shorts, a V-necked T-shirt, and a couple of necklaces and bracelets.*

DARRYL
(*yelling*)

Goddamnit, Thelma, where in the Sam Hell are you?!

EXT. PAY PHONE—DAY

THELMA
(*shakily*)

I'm ... I'm with Louise. We're in the mountains, we're ...

INT. THELMA'S HOUSE—DAY

DARRYL
(*interrupting*)

What in the hell do you think you're doing? Have you lost your goddamn mind?! Is that it? I leave for work and you take complete leave of your senses?

EXT. PAY PHONE—DAY

THELMA

Darryl ... baby ... Darryl, calm down now honey. Please don't get so mad. I can explain ...

INT. THELMA'S HOUSE—DAY

DARRYL *is mad, but he's still watching the game.*

DARRYL

Hold on. Hold on a minute, damnit.

He covers the mouthpiece and watches a play where "his team" fumbles the ball. This only makes him madder. He puts the phone back to his ear in time to hear THELMA say:

THELMA
(*offscreen, on phone*)

. . . only for one day and we'll be back tomorrow night.

DARRYL

No you won't. You'll be back today. Now! You get your ass back here Thelma, now, goddamnit. Thelma, do you understand me?

EXT. PAY PHONE—DAY

THELMA *is trying not to cry. She's trying to be strong.*

THELMA

You're my husband, not my father, Darryl. (*Pleading.*) Darryl, please . . .

INT. THELMA'S HOUSE—DAY

DARRYL
(*interrupting*)

That does it! That Louise is nothin' but a bad influence. If you're not back here tonight goddamnit Thelma . . . well, I just don't wanna say . . .

Neither one of them says anything for a moment.

DARRYL

Thelma?

EXT. PAY PHONE—DAY

THELMA

Darryl.

DARRYL
(*offscreen, on phone*)

What?

THELMA
(*despondent*)

Go fuck yourself.

She hangs up on him. She has tears running down her face and she is watching the ground as she storms back to the car. She makes a loud grunt as she slams into someone that she did not see. Both people are knocked back a few steps from the force of the collision.

HITCHHIKER

Whoa! (*Extremely polite.*) Excuse me! Miss, are you all right?

THELMA shakes her head yes but tears continue. Her crying is silent.

HITCHHIKER
(*very concerned*)

Is there anything I can do?

THELMA shakes her head no. She tries to control her tears. She notices how blue his eyes are.

THELMA

No. Thanks. Sorry.

THELMA collects herself as she walks back to the car. She gets in and is drying her eyes, looking in the side mirror. In the mirror she sees the HITCHHIKER come back around from the side of the building. He is several feet behind the car and she watches him as he removes his long-sleeved shirt and stuffs it into his duffle bag. Now he is just in T-shirt and jeans. He looks good. Really good. She watches in the mirror as he picks up his stuff and heads toward the road. She can see him as he's walking. He stops. He's thinking. He heads over to the car.

HITCHHIKER

Would you mind me asking which direction you and your friend are going? I'm trying to get back to school and my ride fell through, so I'm kind of stuck. Are you going my way?

THELMA doesn't know what to do.

THELMA

Umm. I think we're going to Oklahoma City. But I'm not sure.

HITCHHIKER

Do you think you could . . . I mean, I could help pay for gas.

THELMA knows LOUISE isn't going to like this.

THELMA
(*reticent*)

Ummm. Well, see, it's not really up to me. It's not my car. Umm, we'll have to ask my friend, but she'll probably say no. She's a little uptight.

HITCHHIKER

Well. Maybe we better not ask her. But thank you anyway.

Now she wants him to come. He starts to walk away from the car.

THELMA

Well, we can ask her. That won't hurt.

Just then LOUISE comes out of the store. She sees THELMA talking to this guy and for one moment stops dead in her tracks as she takes this in, then continues toward the car. Although her face is basically expressionless, we see that it's possible she might kill THELMA.

THELMA

Louise, this young man is on his way back to school and needs a ride and I thought since . . .

LOUISE
(*interrupting*)

It's probably not a good idea.

THELMA
(*plaintively*)

Louise.

The hitchhiker just nods and starts walking toward the road.

HITCHHIKER

Y'all have a nice day. Drive safe.

The guy does seem really nice and THELMA is really frustrated that LOUISE wouldn't give him a ride but decides not to confront her.

THELMA

See how polite he is? He was really nice.

LOUISE backs the car out. They watch him walk away. LOUISE pulls out of the parking lot onto the road. They pass the HITCHHIKER. THELMA waves.

HITCHHIKER
(*to* THELMA)

You cheer up now!

She turns around in the seat to continue waving. He smiles and waves. They drive down the road. Tight shot of the HITCHHIKER as the smile fades from his face.

INT. CAR—DAY

DRIVING SHOT. THELMA *looking sulky.*

THELMA

I wish we could've brought him with us.

LOUISE

What did Darryl say?

THELMA
(*sarcastically*)

He said "O.K. THELMA. I just wanted to know you were all right. I hope you're havin' a good time. You sure deserve one after puttin' up with me all the time. I love you honey."

LOUISE doesn't say anything.

THELMA

How long before we're in goddamn Mexico?

INT. POLICE STATION—DAY

HAL *is going over a list of every registered red Impala in the state of Arkansas.* CLOSE SHOT: *computer screen. Names are scrolling by as* HAL *stares blankly at the screen. We see the name* LOUISE ELIZABETH SAWYER *scroll past. It means nothing to* HAL.

EXT. CAR—DAY

DRIVING SHOT. THELMA *is like a dog with a bone. She just won't let it drop.*

THELMA
(*moping*)

I just don't see what it would hurt just to give somebody a ride. Did you see his butt? Darryl doesn't have a cute butt. You could park a car in the shadow of his ass.

LOUISE

I'm sorry. I'm just not in the mood for company right now. Here. Take this map. I need you to find all the secondary roads to Mexico from Oklahoma City. I think we should stay off the interstates. We're too conspicuous.

THELMA
(*taking map*)

Well, it looks like we can get on this road 81 that heads down toward Dallas, then cut over to . . .

LOUISE
(*interrupting*)

I don't want to go that way. Find a way that we don't have to go through Texas.

THELMA
(*looking at map*)

Wait. What? You want to go to Mexico from Oklahoma and you don't want to go through Texas?

LOUISE
(*determined*)

It's crazy, I know, but I . . . you know how I feel about . . . Just find another . . . We're not going that way.

THELMA
(*getting upset*)

I know Louise, but we're running for our lives! Don't you think you could make an exception just this once?! I mean, look at the map. The only thing between Oklahoma and Mexico is Texas!

LOUISE
(*getting flustered*)

Please, Thelma, I know it sounds stupid, but I just don't want to get caught there. If something happens and we get caught, I just don't want it to be there. You understand?

THELMA

No Louise. How come you never said what happened?

LOUISE
(*adamantly*)

Thelma! I'm not gonna talk about this! Now find another way or give me the goddamn map and I will!

LOUISE is completely unreasonable on this subject and THELMA is totally puzzled by LOUISE's reaction but is reluctant to press her further.

LOUISE
(*visibly shaken*)

I . . . I just . . . I just don't think it's the place I wanna get caught for doin' something like . . . If you blow a guy's head off with his pants down, believe me, Texas is the last place you wanna get caught! Trust me! Now, I said, I don't wanna talk about it!!

LOUISE looks very shaken up. She keeps her eyes on the road but she's holding the steering wheel so tightly her knuckles are white. She does not look at THELMA. Suddenly she reaches over and locks her door. THELMA flinches imperceptibly at this gesture.

THELMA
(*quietly*)

O.K. We'll go *around* Texas to get to Mexico. This is crazy.

A truck passes them and the HITCHHIKER waves from the passenger window. THELMA waves back enthusiastically.

THELMA

I'll tell you what. He is gooood lookin'.

LOUISE pops a tape into the dashboard and the piano part begins of Marvin Gaye's version of "Can I Get a Witness."

**OVER MUSIC:**

EXT. LOUISE'S APARTMENT COMPLEX—DAY

HAL *walks up the sidewalk to the door of the apartment complex and knocks.*

**OVER MUSIC:**

INT. LOUISE'S APARTMENT—DAY

VARIOUS SHOTS of LOUISE's empty apartment:

There are pictures of LOUISE and THELMA in high school.
The kitchen is spotless and nothing is out on the counters.
Her bed is unwrinkled, perfect, and next to it on her nightstand is a picture of JIMMY and her in a small heart-shaped frame.
Everything is extremely neat and orderly.

**OVER MUSIC:**

INT. CAR—DAY

DRIVING SHOT. THELMA *and* LOUISE *are singing along with the background vocals of the Marvin Gaye song, both pointing at the radio in a very righteous way.*

THELMA and LOUISE
(*pointing*)

Yeah, yeah, yeah, yeah, yeah, yeah!

EXT. ROAD—DAY

*The* HITCHHIKER *is standing on the side of the road.* THELMA *looks at* LOUISE *pleadingly.* LOUISE*'s car pulls over and he hops in the backseat. An animated* THELMA *turns around backward in the front seat to face him.*

**OVER MUSIC:**

EXT./INT. COFFEE SHOP—DAY

HAL *walks into the coffee shop where* LOUISE *works. Various shots of him talking to other employees:* ALBERT, *waitresses, etc. Some cover their mouths as they recognize police sketches of* LOUISE *and* THELMA. *The day manager comes over, looks at pictures and talks to* HAL.

**OVER MUSIC:**

EXT. CAR—DAY

DRIVING SHOT. THELMA *is passing out beef jerky and Wild Turkey to the* HITCHHIKER *and* LOUISE.

**OVER MUSIC:**

EXT. THELMA'S HOUSE—DAY

HAL*'s unmarked detective car pulls up in front of* THELMA*'s house. A Corvette, completely customized with everything, sits in the driveway.*

EXT. CAR—DAY

DRIVING SHOT. *The* HITCHHIKER *leans over, resting his chin on the back of the front seat.*

THELMA

So J.D., what are you studying in school?

J.D.

Human nature. I'm majoring in behavioral science.

LOUISE
(*cynically*)

And whaddya wanna be when ya grow up?

J.D.

A waiter.

LOUISE laughs. He does have a certain charm.

EXT. THELMA'S HOUSE—DAY

HAL *is walking up the sidewalk as the front door flies open to reveal a drunk* DARRYL *in Hawaiian shorts, necklaces and a beer can in his hand.*

INT. THELMA'S HOUSE—DAY

HAL *and* DARRYL *in den. Pictures and papers are on the table.* TIGHT SHOT *of* DARRYL'S *face.*

DARRYL

What?!

CUT TO: EXTREME CLOSE-UP of DARRYL's face.

DARRYL

What?!!

EXT. RURAL HIGHWAY—DAY

> J.D.
> (*to* THELMA)

So how come you don't have any kids?

> THELMA

Darryl, that's my husband, he says he's not ready. He's still too much of a kid himself. He prides himself on being infantile.

> LOUISE

He's got a lot to be proud of.

> THELMA

Louise and Darryl don't get along.

> LOUISE

That's puttin' it mildly.

> THELMA

She thinks he's a pig.

> LOUISE

He's a real piece o' work. I wish you could meet him.

> J.D.

Did you get married real young?

THELMA

Twenty-four isn't young. I'd already been goin' out with him ten years when we got married. I've never been with anybody but Darryl.

J.D.

Well, if you don' mind my sayin' so, he sounds like a real asshole.

THELMA

It's O.K. He is an asshole. Most of the time I just let it slide.

J.D. is looking down the road, way off in the distance.

J.D.

Better slow down. That's a cop.

LOUISE looks down the road and sees a highway patrol car coming down the road toward them. She does not look alarmed but veers off the road into a "rest area" drive that has trees and shrubs that obscure the view from the road. She glides along as the cop car passes on the other side without seeing them. LOUISE glides right back onto the road as if nothing unusual has happened at all. They realize they have not been spotted. J.D. and LOUISE look at each other.

J.D.

Maybe you got a few too many parking tickets.

LOUISE

We'll take you on to Oklahoma City, then you'd best be on your way.

INT. THELMA'S HOUSE—DAY

HAL *is on the phone to the FBI man.* DARRYL *is sitting on a chair looking dazed. Other law-enforcement types roam around the house.*

HAL

The prints on the trunk of the car match those of Thelma Dickinson.

INT. FBI OFFICE—DAY

MAX STRATTON, *an FBI man in his early forties, is looking at the ident-a-kit drawings of* LOUISE *and* THELMA.

MAX

Well I'll be damned. Isn't that strange.

INT. THELMA'S HOUSE—DAY

HAL

And her husband says a gun is missing. She took a lot of stuff. It looks like she maybe planned on being gone awhile. The strange thing is, her husband said she would never touch that gun. He got it for her 'cause he's out late a lot, but he said she'd never touch it, wouldn't learn to shoot it, just left it in a drawer for years.

INT. FBI OFFICE—DAY

MAX

What kind of gun was it?

HAL
(*offscreen, on phone*)

A thirty-eight.

MAX

Right. Where are they?

INT. THELMA'S HOUSE—DAY

HAL

We're lookin'. They were on their way to some guy's cabin and they never showed up. We're lookin'. We hope you're lookin' too.

EXT. SHADY'S SIESTA MOTEL—DUSK

LOUISE, THELMA *and* J.D. *pull into the motel parking lot.*

LOUISE

I just gotta run in for a minute.

LOUISE looks at J.D. in the backseat and takes the keys out of the ignition.

LOUISE

You two better go on and say your good-byes.

LOUISE gets out of the car and goes inside.

INT. MOTEL OFFICE—DUSK

*An older* WOMAN *behind the counter is looking at a computer screen.*

LOUISE
(*upset*)

Louise Elizabeth Sawyer. Are you sure?

WOMAN

Nothin'. Nothin' come in today at all.

LOUISE turns and sees THELMA crawl over into the backseat with J.D.

LOUISE

Nothing under Peaches? Check again under Peaches.

WOMAN

Naw, nothin' under Peaches neither.

A MAN comes up behind LOUISE and stands close behind her.

MAN

Did you say Peaches?! Why that's the secret word!
Show her what she's won, Don.

He drops an envelope in front of her. LOUISE is startled and turns
around quickly.

JIMMY
(*smiling*)

Hey, Peaches.

LOUISE
(*shocked*)

Oh my God! Jimmy! You . . . Oh my God! What are
you doin' here?

JIMMY
(*to* WOMAN)

Can we get another room? Just put it on my credit card.

The WOMAN hands them a key.

WOMAN

'Round to the back.

EXT. MOTEL PARKING LOT—DUSK

LOUISE *and* JIMMY *walk outside and catch* THELMA *sitting very close to* J.D. THELMA *sees* JIMMY *and is so startled she screams and involuntarily slams herself across the backseat to the other side of the car. She tries to look nonchalant.*

THELMA

Jimmy! Hello stranger. What in the world are you doin' here?

JIMMY
(*smiling*)

Ask me no questions, I'll tell you no lies.

THELMA

Good answer. Same goes double for me.

JIMMY

Who's your friend?

J.D. is already climbing out of the car, looking very uncomfortable.

THELMA

This is J.D. He's a student. We're just givin' him a ride
to . . . to here. Louise said we could bring him here
and then he'd have to go. And that's what he's doin'.
He's goin'. Aren't you, J.D.?

J.D.

Yup. Thanks for the ride. You all take care.

He quickly turns and walks away toward the road.

THELMA
(*watching him*)

Yup. That's him goin'. I love to watch him go.

LOUISE
(*to* JIMMY)

Thelma kinda took to him.

JIMMY is smiling.

JIMMY
(*to* THELMA)

Well, come on, gal, I got you a room. You can go on
in and take a nice cold shower.

THELMA

Don't mind me, Jimmy, I'm just a wild woman.

JIMMY

I always knew that.

THELMA

A regular outlaw.

LOUISE shoots THELMA a look. The three of them drive around to the back of the motel. THELMA turns and looks at the road. J.D. is standing there. He blows her a kiss.

EXT. MOTEL ROOM—DUSK

*They stop in front of the motel rooms and the three of them climb out of the car.*

LOUISE

Let me just go in and freshen up for a minute. I need to wash my face, you know.

THELMA is taking their luggage out of the trunk.

JIMMY

O.K. honey. I don't want to rush you. I just wanna talk to you and (*whispering*) be alone with you. I'll just be in my room, 115, you just come on down when you're ready.

JIMMY helps carry the luggage to THELMA's room. He stops at the door.

JIMMY
(*seductively*)

I'll be waiting.

LOUISE smiles at him quizzically as if she can't believe he's acting this way. He turns on his heel and slinks away.

THELMA

I don't care what you say about him. The boy has got
it bad.

LOUISE

He's always got it bad as long as I'm running in the
other direction. Don't be fooled, he's no different
than any other guy. He knows how to chase and that's
it. Once he's caught you, he don't know what to do.
So he runs away.

THELMA

I heard that.

INT. MOTEL ROOM—DUSK

*They close the door to their room.* LOUISE *sets the envelope of money on the table.*

LOUISE
(*indicating envelope*)

Our future.

LOUISE gets her purse and starts taking out her makeup. She stands
very close to the mirror. She is putting on lip liner. THELMA is watching.

THELMA

So what are you gonna tell him?

LOUISE

Nothing. I'm not gonna tell him a thing. The least I
can do is not make him an accessory any more than
he already is.

THELMA
(*sarcastically*)

You are so sweet to that guy, you really are. Imagine
not wanting to drag him into this. He is a lucky man.

LOUISE is still putting on her makeup, making sure it's perfect.

LOUISE

I didn't ask him to come! It's like I said, Thelma, he
just loves the chase.

THELMA

Well boy he's got his work cut out for him now, don't
he?

LOUISE

Put a lid on it, Thelma! Just let me get this part over
with. Now stay here and guard the money. If there's
any problem I'm in room 115.

THELMA

I won't wait up.

LOUISE turns to face THELMA.

LOUISE

How do I look?

THELMA

You're a vision, Louise, a goddamn vision of loveliness,
you always are.

LOUISE

Have another drink, Thelma.

LOUISE walks out the door.

THELMA

Good idea.

EXT. MOTEL ROOM—NIGHT

LOUISE *knocks on the door to room 115. The door opens slightly and one red rose pops out.*

LOUISE

Hello . . .

JIMMY
(*in a falsetto voice*)

Who is it?

LOUISE

It's me.

The remaining eleven roses are held out the door, then LOUISE is yanked inside and we hear her shriek with laughter.

INT. THELMA'S MOTEL ROOM—NIGHT

THELMA *has taken a shower and is dressed in cutoffs and a T-shirt. Her hair is still damp but she looks better than she did when she arrived.* THELMA *is fixing a drink of Wild Turkey and Diet 7UP in one of the motel room glasses. There is a knock on the door. She stops what she is doing and is completely still.*

THELMA

Louise?

Another knock.

THELMA

Louise, is that you?

J.D.
(*through the door*)

Thelma? It's me.

THELMA opens the door and there stands J.D.

J.D.

I just thought I . . . I know I'm supposed to be gone,
but . . .

He's kind of looking over toward the road. He's still slightly shy.

J.D.

I'm not havin' much luck gettin' a ride.

Looking past her into the room, he notices that LOUISE isn't there.
THELMA just stands there looking at him.

J.D.
(*starting to leave*)

Well, I guess I'd better . . .

THELMA

Wait! . . . Um, where ya goin'?

J.D.

I don't know. Nowhere. What are you doin'?

THELMA

I don't know. Nothin.' Took a shower.

J.D.

That sounds nice.

THELMA

Well, you wanna use the shower?

You can tell he does want to but doesn't want to say so. So instead he just kind of stands there with a reticent grin on his face.

J.D.
(*hesitant*)

Oh. I . . . where's Louise?

THELMA

She's off with Jimmy, that's her boyfriend.

J.D.

That's lonely for you, I guess. I always think of motel rooms as lonely.

THELMA pretends like she's had a lot of experience with this sort of thing.

THELMA
(*letting him in the door*)

Oh, yes, well, they can be.

INT. JIMMY'S ROOM—NIGHT

JIMMY *is pouring champagne into* LOUISE*'s glass. There are a dozen roses in a vase on the table. He pours for himself as he sits as close to* LOUISE *as possible.*

JIMMY

Now, my little coconut, what seems to be the trouble here? Tell Daddy everything.

LOUISE
(*cringing*)

Jimmy, my daddy's still alive and it kind of gives me the creeps when you do that . . .

JIMMY

O.K. O.K., just tell me what's the trouble.

LOUISE just looks at him for a minute.

LOUISE

Jimmy, I'm not gonna tell ya what the trouble is. I don't want ya to get mad and someday soon you'll understand why I can't. But I can't and I won't so don't ask me.

JIMMY is once again shocked by how serious she is.

JIMMY
(*almost at a loss for words*)

O.K., Peaches, O.K. But can I ask you one thing?

LOUISE

Maybe.

JIMMY

Does it have something to do with another guy?

LOUISE

Kind of.

JIMMY

Are you in love with him?

LOUISE

Jimmy, I swear to God, it's nothin' like that.

JIMMY
(*exploding*)

Then WHAT?! WHAT, goddamnit Louise! Where the fuck are you going? Are you just leaving for fucking ever? What, did you fuckin' murder somebody or WHAT?!

LOUISE spills her champagne.

LOUISE

STOP IT! Stop it, Jimmy or I'll leave right now. I'm not kiddin'!

JIMMY
(*calming down*)

All right, all right. I'm sorry.

They both take a second to regain their composure.

JIMMY

Can I just ask you one other thing?

LOUISE

Maybe.

JIMMY

Come here.

LOUISE

You can ask me from there.

JIMMY pulls a little black box out of his pocket.

JIMMY

Will you wear this?

He hands LOUISE the box. She opens it and it is a diamond ring. LOUISE is flabbergasted.

JIMMY

Will you at least see how it fits?

LOUISE

OH MY GOD! Jimmy, oh my . . . it's beautiful! Oh my gosh. I can't believe it!

JIMMY

You didn't see that one comin', did ya?

INT. THELMA'S MOTEL ROOM—NIGHT

J.D. *is out of the shower, standing in front of the mirror wearing only his jeans, the top button of which is still undone, and no shirt. He has an incredible physique. He also has a tattoo on his shoulder of the homemade variety.* THELMA *has gone and bought cheese-crackers and peanuts from a vending machine and is into her second Wild Turkey and 7UP. She sits on the bed, watching him in the mirror. He definitely looks better with his shirt off. She suddenly feels awkward and stands up.*

THELMA

You wanna drink?

INT. JIMMY'S MOTEL ROOM—NIGHT

LOUISE *has the engagement ring on her finger. It's really beautiful.*

JIMMY

So whaddya think? I mean . . . I could . . . get like a job. Like a real job. Of some kind. I mean you've been tellin' me that for years, right?

LOUISE

Why now, Jimmy?

JIMMY

Well try not to get too excited Louise, I just flew across two states with that ring in my pocket and you know how I hate to fly.

LOUISE

You came all this way because you thought I was with somebody else.

JIMMY

No, I didn't. I came because . . . I don't want to lose

you Louise, and for some reason I get the feelin'
you're about to split. Permanently.

                    LOUISE

That's not a reason to get married.

                    JIMMY

I thought that's what you wanted.

                    LOUISE

I did, but not like this.

INT. THELMA'S MOTEL ROOM—NIGHT

THELMA *has poured a drink for* J.D., *who's sitting on the edge of the bed. She
walks over and hands it to him and as she does, he takes the drink with one
hand and her hand with the other. He sets the drink down on the nightstand
and holds her hand with both of his. He closely studies her wedding ring. He
suddenly looks up at her and gazes at her just as intently. He slowly shakes his
head as he removes her ring, as if to say, "This is not right for you. This isn't
going to work." He looks at the ring as he moves it through space finally stopping when the ring is directly over his drink. He drops it in. He looks back at*
THELMA *and smiles as if to say, "There. Now don't you feel better?" He smartly
kisses her hand.*

INT. JIMMY'S ROOM—NIGHT

LOUISE *and* JIMMY *are sitting on the edge of the bed.*

                    JIMMY

You think I'm happy? Playing my one-night gigs in
Ramada Inn lounges . . . and you know . . . You think
you're the only one with dreams that don't work out?

LOUISE

We both got exactly what we settled for.

JIMMY

I think maybe you just don't love me anymore.

LOUISE

No. I do love you. But I think it's time to just . . . let
go of the old mistakes . . . just chalk it up to . . . bad
timing. I think it's time to let go . . .

INT. THELMA'S ROOM—NIGHT

J.D. *is standing on the dresser with a towel tied around his neck like a cape.*

J.D.

Faster than a speeding red Impala, able to leap tall
babes in a single bound . . .

He leaps from the dresser and flies across the room landing on the
bed, straddling THELMA.

J.D.
(*in his deep man's voice*)

Hi. Could I interest you in some Fuller brushes?

THELMA has not stopped laughing since he came in the room. He is
the greatest guy she's ever seen. He is sniffing her neck like a dog.

THELMA
(*giggling*)

Stop, stop, stop!

THELMA tries to catch her breath.

                    THELMA

      Who are you?

J.D. attacks her again.

                         J.D.

      I am the great and powerful Oz . . .

                    THELMA

      J.D.! Just tell me. I know you're not some schoolboy.
      Now come on, nobody ever tells me shit.

                         J.D.

      I'm just a guy. A guy whose parole officer is probably
      having a shit fit right about now.

THELMA gasps.

                    THELMA

      WHAT?! Parole officer? You mean you're a criminal?

                         J.D.

      Well, not anymore, Thelma, except for bustin' parole,
      I haven't done one wrong thing.

                    THELMA

      What'd ya do?

J.D.
(*trying to sound remorseful*)

I'm a robber.

THELMA

You're a bank robber?

J.D.

Nope, I've never robbed a bank.

THELMA

What?

J.D.

Well, I robbed a gas station once, and I robbed a couple of liquor stores, and some convenience stores. And that's it.

THELMA
(*intrigued*)

How?

J.D.

Well, I was just down on my luck and it seemed like somethin' I was good at so I . . .

THELMA
(*interrupting*)

No, I mean how would you do it? Do you just sneak in real fast or hide out till the store closes or what?

J.D.

Naw, honey, that would be burglary. I never got ar-
rested for burglary. Burglary's for chicken shits. If
you're gonna rob someone, ya just have to go right
on up to 'em and do it. Just take the money. That's
robbery. That's a whole 'nother deal.

THELMA

Tell me.

J.D.

Well, first you pick your place, see, then I'd just sit back
and watch it for a while. Ya gotta wait for just the right
moment, which is something you know instinctively,
that can't be taught. Then I'd waltz on in . . .

J.D. jumps up and picks up a hair dryer and holds it like a gun. He
starts acting it out.

J.D.

And I'd say "All right, ladies and gentlemen, let's see
who'll win the prize for keepin' their cool. Simon says
everybody lie down on the floor. If nobody loses their
head, then nobody loses their head. You sir . . . You
do the honors. Just empty that cash into this bag and
you'll have an amazing story to tell all your friends. If
not, you'll have a tag on your toe. You decide." Then
I'd split. Simple.

THELMA

My gosh, you sure were gentlemanly about it.

J.D.

I've always believed if done right, armed robbery doesn't have to be a totally unpleasant experience.

THELMA

God. You're a real live outlaw!

J.D.

I may be the outlaw, but you're the one stealin' my heart.

THELMA

And smooth, boy you are smooth.

They kiss passionately.

J.D.

You're a little angel, you are.

J.D. turns out the light.

INT. JIMMY'S ROOM—NIGHT

LOUISE *and* JIMMY *are wrapped in each other's arms. Through this,* JIMMY *is ardent.*

JIMMY

And do you promise to love, honor and keep me even though I'll probably have no idea where you are or what you're doin' until death do us part?

LOUISE

I do. And do you, Jimmy, take me, Louise, to have and
to hold for the rest of the night, through richness and
poorness and breakfast at the coffee shop until your
plane leaves or it gets light, whichever comes first?

JIMMY is silent for a moment.

JIMMY

I do, darlin'.

They smile and then the smiles fade as the sadness settles on them
and they kiss.

EXT. SHADY'S SIESTA MOTEL—DAWN

MONTAGE *of early morning stuff, a truck driver climbing into his cab with a
silver thermos, squirrels hopping around on the ground.*

INT. SIESTA COFFEE SHOP—DAWN

TIGHT SHOT *of coffee beginning to drip into an empty coffee pot.* LOUISE *and*
JIMMY *are sitting in a booth.*

JIMMY

Don't worry darlin'. I'll say I never found you. I'll say
anything you want. We'll find a way to get you out of
this, whatever it is.

LOUISE

Damn, Jimmy, did you take a pill that makes you say
all the right stuff?

JIMMY

I'm choking on it.

They sit for a minute.

JIMMY

Honey? Ummm . . . Do you want me to come with you?

They look at each other and JIMMY can see that LOUISE is already gone. She is very kind to him.

LOUISE

Ohh . . . now . . . it's probably not a good idea right now. I'll . . . catch up with you later . . . on down the road.

In her hand she's been holding the ring in the black box. She puts it on the table and slides it back to him. He stops her and covers her hand with his.

JIMMY

You keep this.

JIMMY is trying not to seem upset, so he's completely still. A taxi pulls up outside.

LOUISE

Your taxi's here.

JIMMY pulls her to him and kisses her so passionately that employees in the coffee shop look away. A cook fans himself with a spatula. The taxi driver, who can see in, looks at his watch.

JIMMY

Are you happy, Louise? I just want you to be happy.

LOUISE

I'm happy sweetie. Happy as I can be.

JIMMY gets up and leaves the coffee shop. LOUISE watches him go. A waitress comes over and fills her coffee cup.

WAITRESS

Good thing he left when he did. We thought we were gonna have to put out a fire.

The WAITRESS chuckles and the other waitresses do too. LOUISE waves to JIMMY in the back of the cab. The cab driver winks at her. She smiles to herself.

INT. THELMA'S MOTEL ROOM—MORNING

*The room is totally trashed.* J.D. *and* THELMA *are both asleep, naked and hanging off either side of the bed.* J.D. *starts to stir . . .*

INT. HAL'S BEDROOM—MORNING

HAL *is in bed with his wife. He has to get up. He is holding his wife in his arms.*

HAL

Honey?

SARAH

Yes, baby?

HAL

Do you think you could ever shoot someone?

SARAH

What?

HAL

Do you think you could ever think of a set of circum-
stances that would just cause you to haul off and shoot
someone?

SARAH

I could shoot your cousin Eddie.

HAL

Why?

SARAH

Because he's an inconsiderate asshole.

HAL

I'm asking you seriously, Sarah, a stranger?

SARAH

I don't know, honey. I guess it would depend.

HAL

On what?

SARAH
(*trying to picture it*)

Well, maybe if they were trying to hurt you or one of
the kids. I'm sure I could shoot someone if they tried
to hurt one of the children.

HAL

Yeah, I could too. But . . . I don't know why I'm even
asking you this. It's just . . . we can't place anybody at
the scene but these two gals that everybody swears is
sweet as pie.

SARAH

Well, somebody's husband probably got ol' Harlan.

HAL

That's what everybody says. Only problem is nobody's
husband was unaccounted for that night . . . Could you
shoot Eddie in the face? At point-blank range?

SARAH
(*thinking*)

In the leg.

HAL
(*getting up*)

I gotta go to Little Rock.

INT. SIESTA COFFEE SHOP—MORNING

LOUISE *is sitting in the booth by herself.* THELMA *comes hurrying by. She looks
disheveled but is grinning like an idiot. She sees* LOUISE *and charges into the
coffee shop. Her energy and volume are several notches higher than the rest of*

*the people in the coffee shop. There are a couple more customers in there now.*
THELMA *slides into the booth seated directly across from* LOUISE.

>            THELMA
>          (*grinning*)

Hi.

LOUISE is shocked by THELMA's appearance.

>            LOUISE
>          (*sternly*)

What happened to your hair?

>            THELMA
>          (*giddily*)

Nothing. It got messed up.

LOUISE is studying THELMA closely as THELMA squirms in her seat, barely able to contain herself.

>            LOUISE

What's wrong with you?

>            THELMA

Nothing. Why? Do I seem different?

>            LOUISE

Yes, now that you mention it. You seem crazy. Like you're on drugs.

>            THELMA
>          (*barely controlling herself*)

Well, I'm not on drugs. But I might be crazy.

LOUISE
(*shaking her head*)

I don't think I wanna hear what you're gonna tell me.

THELMA is just about to shriek when the waitress comes over and puts a coffee cup on the table and pours some. THELMA gets a grip on herself for a moment then loses it as the waitress goes away.

THELMA

Oh my God, Louise!!! I can't believe it! I just really can't believe it! I mean . . . whoa!

THELMA is just laughing hysterically. LOUISE suddenly understands.

LOUISE

Oh, Thelma. Oh, no.

THELMA

I mean I finally understand what all the fuss is about. This is just a whole 'nother ballgame!

LOUISE
(*embarrassed*)

Thelma, please get a hold of yourself. You're making a spectacle.

THELMA
(*hurt and annoyed*)

You know, Louise, you're supposed to be my best friend. You could at least be a little bit happy for me. You could at least pretend to be slightly happy that for once in my life I have a sexual experience that isn't completely disgusting.

LOUISE

I'm sorry. I am happy. I'm very happy for you. I'm glad
you had a good time. It's about time. Where is he now?

THELMA

Taking a shower.

LOUISE

You left that guy alone in the room?

LOUISE is getting a bad feeling. She is already standing up, putting
money on the table.

LOUISE
(*trying not to sound alarmed*)

Where's the money Thelma?

THELMA has forgotten all about the money.

THELMA

Ummm . . . It's on the table. It's O.K.

They are both leaving the restaurant now. As they hit the door they
both break into a full run.

THELMA

I don't remember.

EXT. MOTEL PARKING LOT—MORNING

They run across the parking lot around the back to the room. The door is ajar and no one is in the room. LOUISE goes in and THELMA stays outside the door.

THELMA

GODDAMNIT! I've never been lucky! Not one time!

LOUISE comes back outside. She doesn't say anything. She is stoic, fighting tears.

THELMA

Shit. That little sonofabitch burgled me. I don't believe it.

LOUISE sits down on the sidewalk in front of the room. THELMA comes and sits beside her. Neither one says anything for a moment. LOUISE starts to cry.

THELMA

Louise? Are you O.K.?

LOUISE shakes her head no.

THELMA
(*completely rattled*)

Louise . . . It's O.K. Louise? I'm sorry. I mean it.

LOUISE has seen the end of the tunnel and there is no light.

LOUISE
(*crying*)

It's not O.K., Thelma. It's definitely not O.K. None of this is O.K. I'm gonna have to sell my ring.

THELMA

No you . . . ring. What ring?

LOUISE holds up her hand for THELMA to see.

THELMA

Oh my God! You mean you got married?!

LOUISE

Just . . . in the room, Thelma. It was purely symbolic, for whatever that's worth.

LOUISE is inconsolable.

THELMA
(*adamantly*)

NO YOU'RE NOT! No you are not either.

LOUISE
(*frustrated*)

Then what are we gonna do for money? What are we gonna buy gas with? Our good looks? I mean . . . goddamn, Thelma!

THELMA

Don't you worry about it. I don't know. I'll take care of it. Just don't you worry about it. Get your stuff.

LOUISE is still sitting on the sidewalk.

THELMA

Come on! Damnit, get your stuff and let's get out of here!

LOUISE slowly gets to her feet.

THELMA

MOVE! (*To herself:*) Jesus Christ, take your damn time.

THELMA is hauling stuff out to the car.

EXT. MOTEL PARKING LOT—MORNING

TIGHT SHOT *of a rear wheel of the red Impala laying rubber out of the motel parking lot.* THELMA *and* LOUISE, *both looking a little rougher than we've seen so far, drive away.*

EXT. THELMA'S HOUSE—MORNING

HAL, MAX (*the FBI Man*) *and various other police and detective types pull up in front of the house. The front door swings open and there stands* DARRYL *looking like he's been shot out of a cannon.*

EXT. STREET—MORNING

LOUISE *and* THELMA *pull into a 7-Eleven.*

INT. THELMA'S HOUSE—MORNING

*Police are tapping the phones, dusting for prints, etc., while* DARRYL *sits motionless in his recliner with a dull expression on his face.*

HAL
(*to* DARRYL)

As you know, we've tapped your phone. In the event that she calls in.

MAX comes up and joins them as they walk down the hallway.

MAX

We're going to leave someone here at the house in the event that she calls in. Someone will be here until we find them.

HAL

The important thing is not to let on that you know anything. We want to try and find out where they are. Now I don't want to get too personal, but do you have a good relationship with your wife? Are you close with her?

DARRYL

Yeah, I guess. I mean I'm as close as I can be with a nutcase like that.

MAX

Well, if she calls, just be gentle. Like you're happy to hear from her. You know, like you really miss her. Women love that shit.

EXT. CONVENIENCE STORE—MORNING

THELMA *and* LOUISE *are sitting in the car. They've put all their money together.*

LOUISE

Eighty-eight dollars ain't gonna make a dent, baby girl.

THELMA
(*getting out of the car*)

Don't worry about it. You want anything?

LOUISE

No.

THELMA marches off to the store. LOUISE puts a tape in the deck and is listening to loud R&B music. She checks herself in the rearview mirror. She takes her lipstick out and is about to put it on. She makes eye contact with herself and instead throws it out the window, closes her eyes and leans her head back on the seat. She's in a world of shit. THELMA comes trotting out of the 7-Eleven and jumps into the car.

THELMA
(*breathless*)

Drive!

LOUISE looks at her.

THELMA

Drive! Drive away!

LOUISE
(*driving away*)

What happened?

THELMA opens her purse and exposes a bag full of bills.

LOUISE

What? You robbed the store? You robbed the god-damn store?!

THELMA shrieks with excitement. LOUISE is completely stunned.

THELMA
(*defensive*)

Well! We need the money! It's not like I killed anybody, for God's sake!

LOUISE shoots her a look. She checks the rearview mirror and looks
back at THELMA as if she has completely lost her mind.

THELMA
(*matter-of-factly*)

I'm sorry. We need the money. Now we have it.

LOUISE
(*getting really scared now*)

Oh shit Thelma!! Shit! Shit! Shit!

THELMA
(*sternly*)

Now you get a grip Louise! Just drive us to goddamn
Mexico, will ya!

LOUISE

O.K. Shit, Thelma! What'd you do? I mean, what did
you say?

THELMA

Well, I just . . .

INT. ARKANSAS STATE POLICE OFFICE—DAY

HAL, MAX, *various other cops and* DARRYL *all watch as a TV plays back a VCR
tape of* THELMA *in the convenience store pulling a gun. In perfect lip sync is:*

THELMA
(*on videotape*)

All right ladies and gentlemen, let's see who'll win the
prize for keepin' their cool. Everybody lie down on
the floor. If nobody loses their head, then nobody
loses their head . . .

CUT TO: TIGHT SHOT of DARRYL's face going deeper and deeper into a
state of shock. Tight shots of HAL, MAX etc., all looking intently at the
screen.

   CUT TO: Videotape image of THELMA boldly ordering cashier to
fill her purse with money. As he's loading the purse with bills, she's
taking beef jerky from the display and putting it in there too, while
she points the gun at the cashier.

THELMA
(*on videotape*)

. . . have an amazing story to tell all your friends. If not,
you'll have a tag on your toe. You decide.

INT. CAR—DAY

THELMA *and* LOUISE *in car, driving.*

LOUISE
(*incredulous*)

Holy shit.

INT. ARKANSAS STATE POLICE OFFICE—DAY

TIGHT SHOT:

DARRYL

Jesus Christ.

CUT TO: TIGHT SHOT:

                         HAL

My Lord.

CUT TO: TIGHT SHOT:

                         MAX

Good God.

EXT. CAR—DAY

DRIVING SHOT.

                    LOUISE

Holy shit.

                    THELMA

Lemme see the map.

LOUISE throws the map across the front seat at THELMA and floors it.


**FADE TO BLACK**


**FADE UP WITH MUSIC**

INT. JIMMY'S APARTMENT BUILDING—DAY

JIMMY *is entering the apartment building, carrying his overnight bag. Two men are sitting on the stairs. They stand as he comes in. They are plainclothes police. They show their badges. He leaves with them.*

EXT. ROAD——DAY


**OVER MUSIC:**

*A tight shot of* J.D.*'s backside, made only more prominent by the bulging wallet in his back right pocket.* J.D. *is walking down the road and continues to walk as an Oklahoma State Patrol car pulls up alongside him. He smiles and gives a friendly wave as they cruise along slowly beside him. We can see the cop nearest him talking and then we see* J.D. *stop walking and set down his duffle bag. He reaches for his wallet. It's clear that they have asked for some I.D.*

EXT. RURAL ROAD——DAY

LOUISE *is driving. They fly past a kid on his bike in a long gravel driveway. He watches them. A huge cloud of dust blows up as they pass him. He turns and rides his bike down the driveway toward the house.*

INT. CAR——DAY

THELMA

Louise, you'd better slow down. I'll just die if we get caught over a speeding ticket.

LOUISE looks at the speedometer touching eighty miles per hour and lets her foot off the gas. LOUISE is looking a little nervous.

LOUISE

For the first time in my life, I wish this car wasn't red.

THELMA

Are you sure we should be driving like this? In broad daylight and everything?

LOUISE

No we shouldn't, but I want to put some distance between us and (*shouting*) the scene of our last goddamn
crime!

THELMA

Oooooweee!! You shoulda seen me! Like I'd been
doin' it all my life! Nobody would ever believe it.

LOUISE

You think you've found your calling?

THELMA

Maybe. Maybe. The call of the wild!

THELMA howls like a dog and drinks a little bottle of Wild Turkey.

LOUISE

You're disturbed.

THELMA

Yes! I believe I am!

INT. ARKANSAS STATE POLICE OFFICE—DAY

JIMMY *is in a small room with* HAL, MAX *and other cops, looking stunned.*

JIMMY
(*shaken up*)

I swear to God, she wouldn't tell me one thing! Christ!
You oughta try to find that kid that was with 'em.

HAL

Tell us about him.

JIMMY

Just some young guy. Around twenty years old. Dark hair.

JIMMY is really upset and has to really struggle to control himself.

JIMMY
(*trying to remember him*)

They said they'd picked him up along the way. He was a student. But he didn't look right. Something wasn't right. But he left when they got to the motel.

MAX

Do you understand that you may be facing an accessory charge?

HAL

This is serious, son. A man is dead.

JIMMY

I know! I'd tell you if I knew! Goddamn! I know something happened or she wouldn't have left. I'm trying to remember everything! Find that fucking kid. He probably knows something.

EXT. CAR——DAY

DRIVING SHOT. THELMA *and* LOUISE *are in the car.* THELMA *is taking empty little Wild Turkey bottles out of her purse and throwing them out the window.*

LOUISE

So what's the plan, Thelma? You just gonna stay drunk?

THELMA

Try to.

LOUISE

Litterbug.

They come roaring up on a semi-tanker carrying gas. We see their fish-eye reflections in the shiny tanker. The mud flaps are the shiny silhouette of a naked woman. There is a bumper sticker on the back that says LICK YOU ALL OVER—TEN CENTS. The truck is going slower than they are.

LOUISE

Aw, great. This always happens. Whenever you're in a hurry.

She noses out to see if she can pass, but there's a car coming. The car passes and the truck honks. The truck driver's arm comes out of his window and waves them past.

LOUISE

Isn't that nice? Truck drivers are always so nice.

THELMA

The best drivers on the road.

As they get next to the truck, the truck driver is smiling and waving at them. They smile and wave back. He flicks his tongue at them. LOUISE screams.

THELMA and LOUISE

UGH!! GROSS! Oh my God! Aw, God!

LOUISE floors it and speeds past him.

THELMA
(*completely grossed out*)

Ugh!! Why do they have to do that?

LOUISE

I guess they think we like it. Maybe they think it turns us on.

LOUISE shivers with disgust.

INT. INTERROGATION ROOM—DAY

JIMMY *is looking at police mug shots of a lot of young guys.* HAL *shows* JIMMY *a mug shot of* J.D.

HAL

Is this the guy you saw them with?

JIMMY
(*looking closely*)

It's him.

MAX
(*clapping his hands*)

Oh happy day.

JIMMY

You gotta be kiddin' me. They picked up a murderer?!

HAL

Armed robber.

JIMMY

Oh, great.

MAX
(*to* HAL)

They're flying him here right now. He was picked up this morning for parole violation. They also found about six grand on him, so he probably knocked over something while he was out there. They can drop him by here for questioning. I'm so happy.

JIMMY
(*overhearing*)

How much cash did he have?

EXT. CAR—DAY

DRIVING SHOT. THELMA *is leaning back in the seat. The radio blares loud R&B music;* THELMA *leans forward and turns the radio down.*

THELMA

Did you ever see that movie about women's prison? The one with Linda Blair?

LOUISE

No, what was the name of it?

THELMA

I don't remember, but there was this one part where
she got on the bad side of some real mean girls. I mean
*really* mean girls, and they got her in the bathroom one
day, when they were supposed to be cleaning the show-
ers and the meanest one, she gets Linda Blair down on
the floor and all her friends are holdin' her down, and
this mean one has this mop handle or this broom handle
and oh my God, it was ugly. I mean she . . . oh my God.

THELMA is too grossed out to go on.

LOUISE
(*also grossed out*)

Thelma! They did not! Where did you see this?

THELMA

On TV!

LOUISE

You did not! They did not show that on TV!

THELMA

It was a damn movie of the week, I swear to God.

LOUISE
(*shocked*)

They can't show that!

THELMA

They didn't actually show it. They'd show Linda Blair
down on the ground, screamin' and cryin', and then

they'd show the mean one bearin' down pretty hard
with this broom handle and oh my God . . .

They both have the creeps.

LOUISE

Oh my God. That girl Linda Blair, she's had some
weird stuff . . . oh my God.

THELMA

They shouldn't show that kind of stuff.

They are both quiet now. They both get very serious. LOUISE pushes
the accelerator to the floor and the car streaks off down the road.

EXT. ARKANSAS STATE POLICE BUILDING—DAY

J.D. *is arriving handcuffed at the State Police building.*

EXT. DIRT ROAD—DAY

LOUISE *and* THELMA *pull off of the main road and drive down a dirt road. A
huge cloud of dust trails behind them.*

THELMA

Louise.

LOUISE

Yeah.

THELMA

I want to call Darryl.

LOUISE

What for?

THELMA

I've been married to the guy for ten years. If I'm gonna run off to Mexico, the least I can do is phone in.

LOUISE

O.K., Thelma. Tonight. But it's risky.

THELMA

Whaddya mean?

LOUISE

I mean if you think he knows anything, you gotta hang up. If he knows, then the police have told him and the phone is probably tapped.

THELMA

Jeez Louise, tapped the phone? You think so?

LOUISE
(*agitated*)

Oh, come on! Murder one and armed robbery, Thelma! They're probably gonna want to talk to us!

THELMA

Murder one! God, Louise, can't we even say it was self-defense?

LOUISE
(*emphatically*)

But it wasn't! We got away! We were walkin' away!

THELMA

They don't know that! It was just you and me there.
I'll say he raped me and you had to shoot him! I mean,
it's almost the truth!

LOUISE

It won't work.

THELMA

Why not?!

LOUISE

No physical evidence. We can't prove he did it. We
probably can't even prove he touched you by now.

They both pause for a moment.

THELMA

God. The law is some tricky shit, isn't it?

Then:

THELMA

How do you know 'bout all this stuff anyway?

LOUISE does not answer the question.

LOUISE

Besides, what do we say about the robbery? No excuse
for that. No such thing as justifiable robbery.

THELMA

All right, Louise!

INT. STATE POLICE BUILDING—LATE AFTERNOON

DARRYL *is sitting in the hallway. Two officers are leading* J.D. *down the hall.*
HAL, MAX *and other plainclothes officers follow.* DARRYL *looks at* HAL *questioningly.* HAL *doesn't respond and the entourage quickly goes into a room.* DARRYL
*stands and crosses the hall to the room as the door shuts in his face.*

DARRYL
(*yelling at the door*)

Hey! HEY!

INT. INTERROGATION ROOM—LATE AFTERNOON

J.D.

Who's that nut?

HAL

That's Thelma Dickinson's husband.

J.D.
(*disgusted*)

Aw, God.

INT. HALLWAY—DAY

DARRYL *tries the doorknob, but the door is locked.*

INT. INTERROGATION ROOM—EVENING

HAL, MAX, J.D. *and other officers are present. There is a VCR and monitor set up in the room and they view the videotape of* THELMA *in the convenience store.*

> J.D.
> (*pleased*)

All right! She did good! Didn't she?

> HAL

Well, son, she's doin' a damn sight better'n you right now.

> MAX

Where did you get sixty-six hundred in cash?

> J.D.

A friend.

> HAL

We spoke with a gentleman today who says he personally delivered very close to that same amount to a Miss Louise Sawyer. Do you know her too?

> J.D.

Umm, yes. She was driving.

> HAL

He said he took it to a motel in Oklahoma City. He also says that at that time, he met a man. He identi-

fied you through a series of mug shots. He also told
us that you and Mrs. Dickinson seemed "close." Is that
true?

J.D.

You might say we had a meeting of the minds, yes.

MAX

Did you know that Mrs. Dickinson and Miss Sawyer are
wanted in connection with a murder?

J.D.

What?!

HAL

Did either one of them ever indicate that they might
be running from the law?

J.D.
(*surprised to hear this*)

Now that you mention it, they might have been a little
jumpy.

HAL

You know what? You're starting to irritate me.

MAX

Yeah. Me too.

HAL thinks for a moment and then looks to MAX.

HAL

Do you mind if I have a word with him alone for a
minute?

MAX agrees and opens the door for everyone to clear out. He and HAL
make eye contact before MAX closes the door.

J.D.

WHAT?! What'd I do?

HAL

Son, I gotta feelin' about something and I just want
to get your opinion. Do you think Thelma Dickinson
would have committed armed robbery if you hadn't
taken all their money?

J.D. doesn't say anything.

HAL

Cat got your tongue?

J.D. shifts in his chair.

J.D.

How do you know I took it? How do you know they
didn't just give it to me?

HAL has had enough.

HAL

There's two girls out there that had a chance, they had
a chance! . . . And you blew it for 'em! Now they've

gotten in some serious trouble and for at least part of it, I'm gonna hold you personally responsible for anything that happens to them. I've got no feelin' for you. But I may be the only person in the world who gives a rat's ass what happens to them and you're gonna tell me every damn thing you know, so that there's a small chance I can actually do them some good, or I'm gonna be all over you like a fly on shit for the rest of your natural life! Your misery is gonna be my goddamn mission in life. That's a sincere promise. Do we understand each other?

J.D.

Yessir.

HAL opens the door and everybody files back in.

J.D.
(*convinced*)

O.K. Is somebody gonna write this down?

INT. HALLWAY—DAY

DARRYL is still sitting in the hallway. HAL comes out of the room first.

HAL

Mr. Dickinson, if you'll just hang on, I want a word with you and then we'll take you on home.

Police officers lead J.D. out of the interrogation room, down the hallway. DARRYL is watching J.D. closely. J.D. is smirking at him.

J.D.
(*slyly, to* DARRYL)

I like your wife.

DARRYL
(*going after him*)

Come back here, you little shit!

HAL and another police officer are restraining DARRYL. J.D. is led off down the hall.

EXT. GAS STATION/MARKET—NIGHT

LOUISE *and* THELMA *pull into a self-serve gas station and market.* LOUISE *goes around to the back of the car and* THELMA *goes in to pay.*

INT. MARKET—NIGHT

*A woman* CLERK *in her forties sits behind the counter reading* Scientific American.

THELMA
(*to the* CLERK)

Twenty dollars on four, and two bags of ice, please.

CLERK

Ice is outside to the right.

As THELMA is getting the money out of her purse she sees the gun there. She stops digging for the money and momentarily spaces out.

CLERK

You want something else?

THELMA snaps out of it.

THELMA

Um, do you have any beef jerky?

The CLERK points to a display about a foot from THELMA's face.

THELMA

Oh. No wonder.

She puts a bag on the counter.

CLERK

Twenty-six oh one. I'll front you the penny if you don't have it.

THELMA

Thanks.

THELMA hands her the money and goes outside.

EXT. GAS STATION—NIGHT

LOUISE *pulls up to the ice freezer and gets out while* THELMA *grabs two bags of ice.* LOUISE *gets out and opens the trunk. They are putting the ice in the cooler.*

LOUISE

There's a phone right over there.

THELMA

Let's get it over with.

They get into the car.

LOUISE

I'm not kidding, Thelma. If you *think* he knows, even if you're not sure, hang up.

They drive across the street to a drive-up pay phone. THELMA dials and begins putting coins into the phone. It rings.

INT. THELMA'S HOUSE—NIGHT

DARRYL, HAL, MAX *and other cops spring into action as the phone rings, putting on headsets, turning on tape recorders.* DARRYL *picks up the phone.*

>                    DARRYL
>
> Hello.

EXT. PAY PHONE—NIGHT

>                    THELMA
>
> Darryl. It's me.

INT. THELMA'S HOUSE—NIGHT

HAL, MAX *et al. are gesticulating wildly.*

>                    DARRYL
>                 (*real friendly*)
>
> Thelma! Hello!

EXT. PAY PHONE—NIGHT

THELMA *hangs up the phone.*

>                    THELMA
>               (*matter-of-factly*)
>
> He knows.

INT. THELMA'S HOUSE—NIGHT

*Everyone is very disappointed, taking off their headsets, turning off tape recorders and looking at* DARRYL *like he's an idiot.*

HAL

Shit.

DARRYL still holds the phone in his hand.

DARRYL

What?! All I said was hello.

EXT. PAY PHONE—NIGHT

THELMA *and* LOUISE *are staring at each other intently.* LOUISE *steps up to the phone.*

LOUISE

You got any change?

THELMA digs in her bag and hands LOUISE a roll of quarters. She puts the money in and dials. It rings.

LOUISE

Darryl, this is Louise. Are the police there?

INT. THELMA'S HOUSE—NIGHT

*Again everybody springs into action.* DARRYL *is fumbling with the phone.*

DARRYL

Uh, NO! No, why would any police be here? Hey, where are you girls anyway?

DARRYL gives HAL and MAX a look as if he's got it completely under control. Clever guy.

EXT. PAY PHONE—NIGHT

LOUISE

Let me talk to whoever's in charge there.

INT. THELMA'S HOUSE—NIGHT

DARRYL

What are you talking about, Louise?

HAL comes over and takes the phone away from DARRYL.

HAL

Hello, Miss Sawyer. I'm Hal Slocumbe, Chief Investigator, Homicide, Arkansas State Police. How are you?

EXT. PAY PHONE—NIGHT

LOUISE

I've been better.

HAL
(*offscreen, on phone*)

You girls are in some hot water.

LOUISE

Yessir. I know.

INT. THELMA'S HOUSE—NIGHT

> HAL

You're both O.K.? Neither one of you hurt? You're bein' careful with that gun?

EXT. PAY PHONE—NIGHT

> LOUISE

We're both fine.

> HAL
> (*offscreen, on phone*)

Good. You wanna tell me what happened?

> LOUISE

Sure. Maybe over coffee sometime. I'll buy.

INT. THELMA'S HOUSE—NIGHT

> HAL

I just want you to know, neither one of you are charged with murder yet. You're still just wanted for questioning. Although now Mrs. Dickinson's wanted in Oklahoma for armed robbery.

EXT. PAY PHONE—NIGHT

> LOUISE

No kiddin'. Listen, we gotta go.

LOUISE looks at her watch.

> HAL
> (*offscreen, on phone*)

Miss Sawyer, I don't think y'all are gonna make it to
Mexico. We should talk.

On hearing this LOUISE mouths the word "shit" in a very frustrated
way. LOUISE hangs up the phone.

INT. THELMA'S HOUSE—NIGHT

*All are busy trying to see if the call was traced.* DARRYL *is back in his recliner
still in shock.*

EXT. PAY PHONE—NIGHT

LOUISE *is stomping back to the car.* THELMA *follows doggedly.*

> LOUISE

That J.D. kid is a little shit.

> THELMA

What?

LOUISE stops as she is about to get in and faces THELMA, who's standing
on the other side of the car.

> LOUISE
> (*terse*)

How'd they find out we're going to Mexico, Thelma,
how do they know that?

THELMA
(*stammering*)

I ... I ...

LOUISE
(*angry*)

You told that thievin' little shit where we were goin?!

LOUISE yanks open her car door, gets in, slams the door and fires up the engine. THELMA hops in quickly.

THELMA
(*whining, defensive*)

I just told him if he ever gets to Mexico to look us up. I asked him not to tell. I didn't think he would tell anybody.

LOUISE

Why not?! What's he got to lose? Other than my life's savings, that is. Shit!

LOUISE careens back onto the road.

THELMA

I'm sorry. I mean I ...

LOUISE slams on the brakes.

LOUISE

Goddamnit, Thelma! Let me explain something to you. Right now we have only two things goin' for us. One, nobody knows where we are and two, nobody knows where we're going. Now, one of our things that was going for us is gone!

LOUISE stops yelling for a moment, groping for self-control. THELMA looks pitiful.

> LOUISE
>
> Just stop talkin' to people, Thelma! Stop bein' so open! We're fugitives now. Let's behave that way!

> THELMA
>
> You're right.

INT. CAR—NIGHT

LOUISE *and* THELMA *drive away. They drive down the road. Neither one of them says anything for a moment.* LOUISE *slaps a tape in.*

> THELMA
> (*tentatively*)
>
> Louise? Where are we?

> LOUISE
>
> Just past Boise City.

> THELMA
>
> Idaho?

> LOUISE
>
> Oklahoma, Thelma. We're crossing into New Mexico.

> THELMA
> (*wistfully*)
>
> I always wanted to see New Mexico.

Thelma's POINT OF VIEW out the passenger-side window is of pitch black-ness.

EXT. BACK ROAD—NIGHT

*The car goes streaking by.*

INT. THELMA'S HOUSE—NIGHT

*All's quiet. The large-screen TV is on and the room is filled with dense smoke.* HAL *and* MAX *sit at a table, going over paperwork. Other plainclothes and surveillance guys play cards.* DARRYL *sits crumpled in his recliner, staring blankly at the TV.*

INT. JIMMY'S HOUSE—NIGHT

JIMMY *sits on his couch with his guitar while two plainclothes cops sit reading the paper, doing the crossword puzzle.*

EXT. CAR—NIGHT

**OVER MUSIC FROM TAPE**

DRIVING SHOT. THELMA *is sipping on a little Wild Turkey.*

THELMA

Now what?

LOUISE

Now what what?

THELMA

Whaddo we do?

LOUISE
(*sarcastically*)

Oh, I don't know Thelma, I guess maybe we could turn ourselves in and spend our lives trading cigarettes for mascara so we can look nice when our families come to visit on Saturdays. Maybe we could have children with the prison guards.

THELMA
(*adamantly*)

I'm not suggesting that! I'm NOT goin' back. No matter what happens. So don't worry about me.

LOUISE speeds up. THELMA hands LOUISE a little bottle of Wild Turkey and she drinks it down. THELMA has one too.

THELMA

Can I ask you kind of a weird question?

LOUISE

Yeah.

THELMA

Of all the things in the world that scare you, what's the worst thing that scares you the most?

LOUISE

You mean now or before?

THELMA

Before.

LOUISE

I guess I always thought the worst thing that could happen would be to end up old and alone in some crummy apartment with one of those little dogs.

THELMA

What little dogs?

LOUISE

You know those little dogs you see people with?

THELMA

Like a Chihuahua?

LOUISE

Those too, but you know those little hairy ones? Those flat-faced little fuckers with those ugly goddamned teeth?

THELMA

Oh yeah. You mean Peek-a-poos.

LOUISE

Yeah. Those. That always put the fear of God in me. What about you?

THELMA

Well, to be honest, the idea of getting old with Darryl was kinda startin' to get to me.

LOUISE

I can see that.

THELMA

I mean, look how different he looks just since high school. It's bad enough I have to get old, but doin' it with Darryl around is only gonna make it worse. (*Quieter.*) I mean, I don't think he's gonna be very nice about it.

LOUISE

Well, now maybe you won't have to.

THELMA

Always lookin' on the bright side, aren't ya?

EXT. MOONLIT DESERT HIGHWAY—NIGHT

*A song by Pat McLaughlin called "In a Moment of Weakness" plays.*

> SONG: . . . *Still in a moment of weakness, I'll fly away*
> *Up on the wings of some holy bird, out on that sunshiny day*
> *Forgive me for being so ungrateful, and I'm about half of alive*
> *Still in a moment of weakness, only the strong will survive . . .*

*They are driving through Monument Valley. The Impala speeds through the beautifully moonlit desert. It is almost like daylight.*

EXT. DESERT—NIGHT

**OVER MUSIC:**

*A shot of the full moon rising. A montage of silhouettes of cacti, huge rock formations, desert beauty shots, etc.*

INT. CAR—NIGHT

LOUISE *and* THELMA'S POINT OF VIEW *is through the windshield. The sky is bright and expansive and the road goes on forever.*

THELMA

This is so beautiful.

LOUISE
(*awestruck*)

Gosh. It sure is.

THELMA

I always wanted to travel. I just never got the opportunity.

LOUISE

You get what you settle for.

THELMA

What's that supposed to mean?

LOUISE

Nothin'. Keep a lookout for UFOs.

They both look forward for another moment. And then at the same time they look at each other, each taking the other one in completely, in this moment. They're saying everything to each other in this moment, but their expressions don't change and they don't say a word. Pat McLaughlin sings on the radio.

EXT. DESERT HIGHWAY—NIGHT

*A semi-tanker is up ahead on the road. It looks like the one they saw earlier. It's got the same mud flaps . . .*

INT. CAR—NIGHT

>                    LOUISE
>
> Look! Look who it is, Thelma. I'll be darned. What's he doin' way out here?

>                    THELMA
>
> Just ignore him.

LOUISE passes him and as she does he honks. They look up and he is wildly pointing to his lap.

>                    LOUISE
>
> Oh, Christ. I hate this guy.

>                    THELMA
>
> We should have just ignored him.

EXT. DESERT HIGHWAY—NIGHT


**OVER MUSIC:**

*The car is flying down the road.*

INT. THELMA'S HOUSE—NIGHT

*There is one light on in the den.* HAL *is the only one awake in a room full of men sleeping with their mouths wide open.*

INT. JIMMY'S APARTMENT—DAWN (FIRST LIGHT)

*The room is blue, with the sky outside just beginning to get light.* MAX *is now at* JIMMY'*s apartment. The policemen are asleep.* JIMMY'*s phone rings. Everyone leaps up.*

INT. THELMA'S HOUSE—DAWN (FIRST LIGHT)

*Everyone springs back to life there, too.* HAL *grabs his headset.*

                    SURVEILLANCE MAN

It's at the other place.

INT. JIMMY'S APARTMENT—DAWN (FIRST LIGHT)

JIMMY *answers the phone.*

                         JIMMY

Hello.

                        LOUISE
                (*offscreen, on phone*)

Hey darlin'. Guess who?

EXT. CLOSED GAS STATION—DAWN (FIRST LIGHT)

LOUISE *is on the pay phone at an old gas station.*

                        LOUISE

Are the cops on your phone? I guess they are. Hey
everybody, can I talk to Jimmy alone for a second? I'm
not gonna say anything 'bout where we are, and I'm
not gonna talk long enough for you to trace it.

INT. THELMA'S HOUSE—DAWN

HAL

O.K., Miss Sawyer. But please talk to me. I want to help
you.

LOUISE
(*impatiently*)

Then I'll call you back.

EXT. CLOSED GAS STATION—DAWN

LOUISE *looks at her watch.* THELMA *goes into the restroom but comes out immediately, thoroughly disgusted. She clambers down the embankment to find a
spot out of sight.*

INT. JIMMY'S APARTMENT—DAWN

JIMMY

O.K. They're off over here. I can't believe this is happening.

LOUISE

Wild, isn't it? I just want to say I'm sorry about all this.
I love you. I miss you. I'll love you forever.

JIMMY

Same goes double for me, Peaches.

EXT. GAS STATION—DAWN

LOUISE *is looking at her watch.* THELMA *is back, just leaning on the car watching* LOUISE. *She studies her as if she's never really seen her before.* LOUISE *is
oblivious. She is wrapped up, traveling through the wires.*

LOUISE

I'm makin' a terrible wife, aren't I?

INT. JIMMY'S APARTMENT—DAWN

JIMMY
(*smiling*)

Where's my dinner, sweetie?

EXT. CLOSED GAS STATION—DAWN

LOUISE *hangs up the phone. She stands for a moment, lost in thought.*

INT. THELMA'S HOUSE—DAWN

HAL *takes off the headset and looks at the* SURVEILLANCE MAN, *who shakes his head, indicating it wasn't enough time, they didn't get it.*

EXT. CLOSED GAS STATION—DAWN

LOUISE *is walking back to the car, a bare smile left on her face.* THELMA *watches. All of a sudden, a look of shocked realization comes over* THELMA*'s face. It startles* LOUISE.

LOUISE

What.

THELMA
(*carefully*)

It happened to you . . . didn't it?

LOUISE knows what she is talking about. She becomes immediately agitated.

LOUISE

I don't want to talk about it! Thelma, I'm not kidding!
Don't you even . . .

THELMA

. . . in Texas . . . didn't it? That's what happened . . .
Oh my God.

LOUISE
(*vehemently*)

Shut up! Shut up goddamnit, Thelma! You just shut
the fuck up.

LOUISE looks as if she is looking for a way to flee. She opens the car
door and then slams it closed. She paces around the car.

THELMA
(*quietly, almost to herself*)

Now I see . . . that's what happened.

LOUISE
(*through clenched teeth*)

I'm warning you, Thelma. You better drop it right
now! I don't want to talk about it!

THELMA
(*gently*)

O.K. Louise . . . It's O.K.

LOUISE's eyes are wild, not seeing, while THELMA now seems completely
serene. They are quiet for a moment, then THELMA starts quietly laughing to herself. She is trying to stop but cannot.

LOUISE

What?

THELMA
(*shaking with laughter*)

Nothing. It's not funny.

LOUISE

What? What's not funny, Thelma!

THELMA is trying to compose herself but cannot.

THELMA

O.K. but . . . (*she can barely speak*) I can't say.

THELMA isn't making a sound. She is stuck in a convulsion of laughter.

LOUISE

What?!

THELMA
(*gasping for air*)

Harlan.

LOUISE

What?! What about him?!

THELMA

Just the look on his face when you . . . (*She is falling apart again.*) It's not funny!

> LOUISE
> (*shocked*)

Now Thelma, that is not . . .

THELMA is still trying to get a grip on herself.

> THELMA

Boy, he wasn't expectin' that!

> LOUISE
> (*scolding*)

Thelma!

> LOUISE
> (*impersonating* HARLAN)

Suck my dick . . . BOOM!!

THELMA is laughing wildly.

> LOUISE
> (*quietly*)

Thelma. It's not funny.

THELMA has just crossed the line from laughing to crying.

> THELMA
> (*trying to catch her breath*)

I know!

They both get quiet.

EXT. DESERT HIGHWAY—DAWN

**OVER MUSIC:**

*The car is screaming down the road. They drive through a little stand of buildings. As they whiz past the buildings, a set of car headlights pop on. A car pulls out onto the road and follows them. The car speeds up to try to catch them. The red and blue lights pop on. It is a New Mexico State Patrol car.*

INT. CAR—DAWN

LOUISE *sees the lights in the rearview mirror.* LOUISE*'s point of view is of the speedometer at one hundred miles per hour.* THELMA *is asleep.*

LOUISE

Shit! Thelma, wake up! Shit! We're gettin' pulled over!

THELMA jumps awake.

THELMA

What! What! Oh shit! Oh no!

They are trying not to panic. They are slowing down but still doing seventy miles per hour. The patrol car is right behind them.

THELMA

What do we do? What do you want to do?!

LOUISE

I don't know! Shit! Let's just play it by ear. He may not know. He may just give me a ticket.

THELMA

Please, God, please don't let us get caught. Please, please, please . . .

LOUISE pulls the car off the road. The patrol car pulls up right behind them. The lights shine brightly in through the windows.

EXT. SIDE OF DESERT HIGHWAY—EARLY MORNING

> PATROLMAN
> (*over bullhorn*)

## TURN OFF YOUR ENGINE.

LOUISE does. The PATROLMAN gets out of his car and approaches them, shining his flashlight into the car. He comes to the driver's side window. It is rolled up. The PATROLMAN's point of view is of LOUISE smiling up at him. He gestures to her to roll her window down. She does.

> LOUISE
> (*friendly*)

Hello, officer. Is there a problem?

> PATROLMAN

You wanna let me see your license please?

LOUISE fumbles in her purse for her wallet, opens it and shows her license.

> PATROLMAN

You wanna take it out of your wallet please?

> LOUISE

Oh yeah.

She does and hands it to him.

THELMA

I told you to slow down. Hell, officer. I told her to slow
down.

LOUISE
(*polite*)

About how fast was I going?

PATROLMAN

About a hundred and ten. You wanna step out of the
car please?

They walk to the back of the car. He shines the flashlight on the license
plate.

PATROLMAN

Is this your car?

LOUISE

Yes.

PATROLMAN

You wanna come with me please? Walk around and
get in the car please.

LOUISE

In the back?

PATROLMAN

Front.

LOUISE

Am I in trouble?

PATROLMAN

As far as I'm concerned, yes ma'am, you are.

The PATROLMAN gets in the driver's side. He picks up a clipboard and clips LOUISE's driver's license to it. He picks up the hand mike for the radio and as he does, a hand with a gun comes in his car window. It's THELMA and she puts the gun to his head.

THELMA
(*sincerely*)

Officer, I am so sorry about this. Could you let go of that?

He drops it.

THELMA

I really, really apologize but please put your hands on the steering wheel. See, if you get on that radio, you're gonna find out that we're wanted in two states and probably considered armed and dangerous, at least I am, then our whole plan would be shot to hell. Louise, take his gun.

LOUISE, in a complete state of shock, reaches over and takes his gun.

LOUISE
(*apologetic*)

I am really sorry about this.

THELMA

I swear, before yesterday, neither one of us would have
ever pulled a stunt like this. But if you ever met my
husband, you'd know why I just can't . . . You wanna
step out of the car please?

She opens the door for him.

THELMA

You wanna put your hands on your head please?
Louise, shoot the radio.

LOUISE

What?

THELMA

Shoot the radio!

LOUISE shoots the car radio. The cop flinches with each shot.

THELMA
(*exasperated*)

The police radio, Louise! Jesus!

LOUISE fires two shots into the police radio. It blasts it all to hell.

THELMA

You wanna step to the back of the car please. Louise,
bring the keys.

LOUISE reaches over and takes the keys. She takes her license off the
clipboard. She gets out and trots around to the back of the car. THELMA

is holding the gun on the PATROLMAN. Suddenly THELMA fires the gun, blowing two holes into the trunk cover.

                    THELMA
                   (*to* LOUISE)

Open the trunk.

LOUISE opens the trunk.

                    THELMA
                (*to* PATROLMAN)

You wanna step into the trunk please?

                  PATROLMAN
                 (*really scared*)

Ma'am, please . . . I've got kids . . . a wife.

                    THELMA

You do? Well you're lucky. You be sweet to 'em. Especially your wife. My husband wasn't sweet to me and look how I turned out. Now go on, get in there.

As he's climbing into the trunk, THELMA explains to LOUISE:

                    THELMA

Air holes.

He's all the way in and LOUISE closes the trunk.

INT. PATROL CAR—DAWN

THELMA *gets into the car and opens the glove compartment. She takes a box of spare ammo and closes it.* THELMA *takes the keys and gets out of the car. She walks around to the trunk.*

EXT. PATROL CAR—DAWN

>                    THELMA
>                   (*to trunk*)

Sorry!

>                    LOUISE
>                  (*from her car*)

Sorry!

THELMA hops into the car with LOUISE. They look at each other.

>                    LOUISE

Ready?

>                    THELMA

Hit it.

LOUISE pulls the car back onto the road and they drive away.

INT. CAR—MORNING

>                    THELMA
>                (*shaking her head*)

I know it's crazy Louise, but I just feel like I've got a
knack for this shit.

>                    LOUISE

I believe you

EXT. DESERT ROAD—MORNING

*The car goes streaking by.*

THELMA
(*voice-over*)

Drive like hell.

A MONTAGE OF DRIVING SHOTS. They are in really beautiful country now.

THELMA

Louise?

LOUISE

Yes?

THELMA

Where are we?

LOUISE

Colorado.

THELMA

Um. Isn't Colorado north of New Mexico?

LOUISE

Yes it is.

THELMA

Are we still going to Mexico?

LOUISE

Yes.

THELMA pauses while she searches for the logic.

THELMA

Then aren't we going in the wrong direction?

LOUISE

Well, we were so close to the border, and I figure when you take a state policeman, shoot up his car, take his gun and lock him in the trunk, it's best to just get on out of the state if you can.

THELMA

Just asking.

They are both quiet for a second. LOUISE goes a little faster.

INT. JIMMY'S APARTMENT—MORNING

MAX *is on the cellular phone there.*

MAX

It's just not working like this. We gotta do something. It'd be one thing if these girls were hardened criminals, but Jesus, Hal, this is makin' us look bad. I don't know . . . maybe they're not movin'. Maybe that little creep lied.

HAL
(*offscreen, on phone*)

He's got nothin' to gain by lyin'. Nothin' at all. He already got all their money.

INT. THELMA'S HOUSE—MORNING

> HAL

> I just don't know what we're dealin' with here. I'll tell you one thing. I don't want anybody losin' their heads. You know what happens. The volume gets turned way up and the next thing you know those girls are gonna get shot. Anyway, it went out again last night on nationwide teletype. Let's just wait it out a little longer. She said she was gonna call back. Let's just sit tight.

INT. JIMMY'S APARTMENT—MORNING

> MAX

> We don't have a whole lotta choice, do we? I can't figure out if they're real smart or just really, really lucky.

> HAL
> (*offscreen, on phone*)

> It don't matter. Brains will only get you so far and luck always runs out.

INT. CAR—MORNING

THELMA *is digging through her bag.*

> LOUISE

> Don't you hand me another piece of beef jerky, you hear.

> THELMA

> What do you mean?

LOUISE

I mean the next beef jerky you hand me is goin' out
the window. I don't want to see any more beef jerky.
It's drivin' me crazy. The whole car smells like it.

THELMA

It's good. It's what the pioneers ate.

LOUISE

I don't care what the damn pioneers ate. You just keep
that shit away from me, now I mean it.

THELMA puts down her bag.

LOUISE

And I don't want any more Wild Turkey, either. It's
burning a hole in my stomach.

THELMA

O.K., O.K. . . . I've got some tequila. You want some tequila?

LOUISE

You do?

THELMA

Yeah, you want it?

LOUISE

Yeah.

THELMA starts to dig through her bag again.

> THELMA
>
> It's in here somewhere.

LOUISE is rubbing her face. She looks pretty bad. Her hands are shaking.

> LOUISE
> (*to herself*)
>
> Shit. I'm gettin' tired.

> THELMA
>
> Are you all right?

LOUISE does not really seem all right.

> LOUISE
> (*upset*)
>
> I think I've really fucked up. I think I've got us in a situation where we could both get killed. I mean, I don't know what's the matter with me. I don't know why we didn't just go straight to the police.

> THELMA
>
> You know why. You already said.

> LOUISE
>
> What'd I say?

> THELMA
>
> Nobody would believe us. We'd still get in trouble.

We'd still have our lives ruined. And you know what else?

                    LOUISE

What?

                    THELMA

That guy was hurtin' me. And if you hadn't come out when you did, he'd a hurt me a lot worse. And probably nothin' woulda ever happened to him. 'Cause everybody did see me dancin' with him all night. And they woulda made out like I asked for it. And my life woulda been ruined a whole lot worse than it is now. At least now I'm havin' fun. And I'm not sorry that son of a bitch is dead. I'm only sorry that it was you that did it and not me. And if I haven't, I wanna take this time to thank you, Louise. Thank you for savin' my ass.

                    LOUISE

I said all that?

                    THELMA

No, Louise, you said the first part. I said all the rest.

                    LOUISE
                    (*tired*)

Whatever.

EXT. PAY PHONE—MORNING

LOUISE *is at a pay phone as the sky is just starting to get light.* THELMA *is in the bathroom nearby.* LOUISE *has already dialed and the phone is ringing.*

INT. THELMA'S HOUSE—MORNING

*As the phone rings, everyone leaps into action again.* HAL *picks up the phone.*

> HAL

Hello.

INT. JIMMY'S APARTMENT—MORNING

MAX *is listening through a headset.* JIMMY *is watching intently.*

EXT. PAY PHONE—MORNING

> LOUISE

Hey.

> HAL
> (*offscreen, on phone*)

How are things goin' out there?

> LOUISE

Weird. Got some kind of a snowball effect goin' here or somethin'.

> HAL
> (*offscreen*)

You're still with us though. Somewhere on the face of the earth?

> LOUISE

Well, we're not in the middle of nowhere, but we can see it from here.

INT. THELMA'S HOUSE—MORNING

HAL *smiles.*

> HAL
>
> I swear, Louise, I almost feel like I know you.

> LOUISE
> (*offscreen, on phone*)
>
> Well. You don't.

> HAL
>
> You're gettin' in deeper every moment you're gone.

> LOUISE
> (*offscreen, laughs despondently*)
>
> Would you believe me if I told you this whole thing is an accident?

> HAL
>
> I do believe you. Trouble is, it doesn't look like an accident and you're not here to tell me about it . . .

EXT. PAY PHONE—MORNING

LOUISE *does not answer.*

> HAL
> (*offscreen, on phone*)
>
> Did Harlan Puckett . . .

> LOUISE
> (*interrupting*)
>
> No!

HAL
(*offscreen*)

You want to come on in?

LOUISE thinks for a minute.

LOUISE

I don't think so.

INT. THELMA'S HOUSE—MORNING

HAL
(*quietly*)

Then I'm sorry. We're gonna have to charge you with murder. Now, do you want to come out of this alive?

The SURVEILLANCE MAN motions to HAL to keep it going.

EXT. PAY PHONE—MORNING

LOUISE

You know, certain words and phrases keep floating through my mind, things like incarceration, cavity search, life imprisonment, death by electrocution, that sort of thing. So, come out alive? I don't know. Let us think about that.

A finger reaches up and presses down the lever and hangs up the phone.

INT. THELMA'S HOUSE—MORNING

*Frustrated,* HAL *slams down the phone. He looks over at the* SURVEILLANCE MAN *who nods as if to say "We got it." The entire room springs into action.*

MAX *immediately picks up the phone and* HAL *watches him intently. He mouths to* MAX *the words "I wanna go," emphatically.* MAX *nods affirmatively.*

EXT. PAY PHONE—MORNING

ANGLE ON THELMA. *She has her finger on the lever.*

> THELMA
>
> Come on Louise. Don't blow it. Let's go.

She walks away toward the car. LOUISE is still standing there holding the phone. THELMA stops and looks at her.

> THELMA
>
> Come on.

LOUISE doesn't move.

> THELMA
>
> Louise?

> LOUISE
>
> Yes, Thelma?

> THELMA
>
> You're not gonna give up on me, are ya?

> LOUISE
>
> What do you mean?

THELMA

You're not gonna make some deal with that guy are you? I mean, I just wanna know.

LOUISE

No, Thelma. I'm not gonna make any deals.

THELMA

I can understand if you're thinkin' about it. I mean, in a way, you've got something to go back for. I mean Jimmy and everything.

LOUISE is surprised to be hearing this from THELMA.

LOUISE

Thelma, that is not an option.

THELMA

But, I don't know . . . something's crossed over in me and I can't go back. I mean, I just couldn't live . . .

LOUISE

I know. I know what you mean. I don't wanna end up on the damn *Geraldo* show.

They are both quiet for a moment.

LOUISE

He said they're gonna charge us with murder.

>                THELMA
>             (*making a face*)

Eeuww.

>                LOUISE

And we have to decide whether we want to come out of this dead or alive.

>                THELMA
>             (*exasperated*)

Gosh, didn't he say anything positive at all?

LOUISE starts the car. They lurch into reverse then screech forward as they tear off down the road. We see a wide shot of the car as they drive away.

INT. CAR—DAY

>                THELMA
>             (*concerned*)

Louise, do you think we should change cars, get another car?

>                LOUISE

How do you suggest we go about that? Steal one? You know how to hot-wire a car?

>                THELMA

No.

>                LOUISE

Well, don't worry. I'm sure you'll figure it out.

EXT. AIRSTRIP—DAY

**OVER MUSIC:**

*A car pulls up on the airstrip and stops next to a small jet.* HAL *and* MAX *get out of the car and board the plane.*

EXT. DESERT—DAY

A MONTAGE OF DRIVING SHOTS *as* LOUISE *and* THELMA *drive through the intense beauty of the Arizona desert.*

INT. CAR—DAY

>                    THELMA
>
> You awake?

>                    LOUISE
>
> You could call it that. My eyes are open.

>                    THELMA
>
> Me too. I feel awake.

>                    LOUISE
>
> Good.

>                    THELMA
>
> Wide awake. I don't remember ever feelin' this awake.
> Everything looks different.

>                    LOUISE
>
> You've never been here before.

THELMA

You know what I mean. I know you know what I mean. Everything looks new. And I feel like I've got something to look forward to. Do you feel like that? Like you've got something to look forward to?

LOUISE

I guess I just feel . . . busy.

THELMA

I guess that's it.

LOUISE
(*seriously*)

We're up to our ass in alligators.

THELMA

Well, try to look at the bright side. At least you don't have to go to work tonight.

This gets a smile out of LOUISE.

THELMA

Are you gonna call 'em and tell 'em you're not coming in?

LOUISE

Can you do that? Call in psychotic? "Hi, it's Louise. I've had a complete mental breakdown. Can you get someone to cover my shift?"

"We think you should apologize."

"Why don't you ditch that loser husband of yours?"

"Darryl . . . go fuck yourself!"

Brad Pitt as good-looking con
artist J.D.

"Is the manager in?"

"My husband wasn't sweet to me and look how I turned out."

"But I can't go back . . . I mean, I just couldn't live."

"Go."

The King family

"You trying to humiliate your whole goddam family?"

"Honey, he slipped."

*Something to Talk About* © 1995 Warner Bros., a division of
Time Warner Entertainment Company, L.P

"I was just wondering if anybody else here has fucked my husband!"

"And, Wyly, you fart in your sleep!"

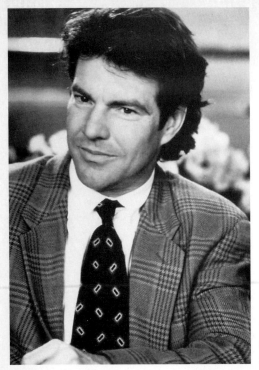

"You know, Eddie, maybe someday you and Grace will make fantastic grown-ups."

That's the thing you gotta love about Daddy, even when he loses, he wins."

*Something to Talk About* © 1995
Warner Bros., a division of
Time Warner Entertainment
Company, L.P

This cracks them up.

LOUISE

"Hi, Eddie, I'm off on a crime spree so will you see if Cheryl wants my section?"

LOUISE and THELMA both get quiet for a second.

LOUISE

We'll be drinkin' margaritas by the sea, mamacita.

THELMA

We can change our names.

LOUISE

We can live in a hacienda.

THELMA

I wanna get a job. I wanna work at Club Med.

LOUISE

Yes! Yes! Now what kind of deal do you think that cop can come up with to beat that?

THELMA

It'd have to be pretty good.

LOUISE

It would have to be pretty damn good.

They are both laughing. The car is still flying down the road. The sun is coming up higher in the sky now. They come to an intersection in the middle of nowhere. LOUISE stops and looks at the map.

> LOUISE
>
> I'm gonna head a little further in. There's not that many roads in this state. I want to try to hit Mexico somewhere not so close to New Mexico. They probably wanna kill us in New Mexico.

> THELMA
>
> You're drivin'.

LOUISE takes a right turn and speeds down the road.

EXT. ROAD—DAY

LOUISE *and* THELMA *are singing along to a wild R&B song. They do the hand movements as if they are the Supremes. They come roaring up on the semi-tanker, the same one they have seen twice before now.*

> THELMA
> (*screaming over music*)
>
> Oh my God! Louise! Look! Look! See if it's him!

> LOUISE
>
> It's him. He's got California plates. It's the same guy.

> THELMA
>
> Pass him!

LOUISE bears down really hard and passes him. Again as they get right next to him, he blows kisses down at them. He is leering at them and laughing. LOUISE and THELMA drive further down the road. LOUISE pulls the car off to the side of the road. As the truck gets close they start waving to him to stop. He pulls his truck off the side of the road and stops. Angle on LOUISE and THELMA smiling up at him. He chuckles to himself. He leans out the window.

THELMA

Hi!

TRUCKER

Hi there! You all all right?

THELMA

We're fine! How are you?

TRUCKER

Grrrreat!

LOUISE

Come talk to us.

INT. TRUCK CAB—DAY

*The* TRUCKER *reaches over and opens a glove compartment crammed full of condoms. He grabs a few and shoves them in his pocket. He turns off his engine and gets out of the truck.*

EXT. SIDE OF ROAD—DAY

*He walks up to the car.* THELMA *and* LOUISE *are sitting on the back of the car seats.*

THELMA

Where you goin'?

TRUCKER

Fresno.

LOUISE

We been seein' you all along the way.

TRUCKER

Yeah, I been seein' you too.

THELMA

We think you have really bad manners.

LOUISE nods.

LOUISE

We were just wonderin' where you think you get off
behavin' like that to women you don't even know.

This is not what is supposed to be happening.

TRUCKER

What? What are you talkin' about?

LOUISE

You know good and damn well what I'm talkin' about.

THELMA

I mean really! That business with your tongue. What is that? That's disgusting!

LOUISE

And, oh my God, that other thing, that pointing at your lap? What's that supposed to mean exactly? Does that mean pull over, I want to show you what a big fat slob I am or . . .

THELMA

Does that mean suck my dick?

TRUCKER

You women are crazy!

LOUISE

You got that right.

THELMA

We think you should apologize.

He is getting a little panicky.

TRUCKER
(*scared*)

I'm not apologizing for shit!

LOUISE

Just say you're sorry.

TRUCKER

Fuck that.

LOUISE pulls the gun they stole from the state patrolman.

LOUISE

Say you're sorry or we'll make you fuckin' sorry.

His hands fly up in the air.

TRUCKER

Oh, Jesus!

THELMA

You probably even called us beavers on your CB radio, didn't you?

He nods, still repeating the words.

THELMA

Damn. I hate that! I hate bein' called a beaver, don't you?

LOUISE

Are you going to apologize or not?

TRUCKER
(*scared shitless*)

Fuck you!

LOUISE looks at his truck off in the distance. She points the gun at it, takes a second to get a bead, then shoots two of the tires flat. The truck slowly sinks as the air escapes from the tires.

TRUCKER
(*devastated*)

Oh goddamn!! You bitch!!

LOUISE and THELMA look at each other. They both turn toward the truck and fire rounds into the tanker until it explodes in a huge ball of fire. The TRUCKER screams at the top of his lungs. LOUISE starts the car and starts driving in circles around the TRUCKER. THELMA and LOUISE are both howling at the top of their lungs. THELMA is sitting on the back of the front seat with her feet on the dashboard.

TRUCKER

You fucking bitch! AAAaaaarrrgghh!!! You're gonna have to pay for that!!! I'm gonna make you PAY for that!! You hear me??!!

LOUISE stops the car right next to him.

THELMA

Shut up.

LOUISE takes off again and THELMA falls into the backseat. They drive off trailing a huge cloud of dust.

INT. CAR—DAY

THELMA *pops up from the backseat.*

THELMA

Hey. Where'd you learn to shoot like that?

> LOUISE

Texas.

EXT. DESERT—DAY

LOUISE *drives through the desert back toward the road, past the burning debris of the truck. As she gets to the road she stops.* THELMA *climbs into the front seat.*

INT. CAR—DAY

*As* THELMA *and* LOUISE *talk, their voices are heard over the following scenes.*

> LOUISE
> (*voice-over*)

You know what's happened, don't you?

> THELMA
> (*voice-over*)

What?

> LOUISE
> (*voice-over*)

We've gone insane.

> THELMA
> (*voice-over*)

Yup.

EXT. ROAD—DAY

*The car careens back onto the road, missing the burning debris.*

EXT. NEW MEXICO; SIDE OF ROAD—DAY

*A battered pickup truck is parked by the New Mexico State Patrol car. An old man uses a crowbar to pry open the trunk. The* PATROLMAN *hops out of the trunk.*

EXT. DESERT ROAD—DAY

HELICOPTER SHOT. *A police helicopter flies over the burning wreckage of the semi-tanker. The* TRUCKER *is waving his arms as the helicopter descends, blowing dirt all over him.*

INT. THELMA'S HOUSE—DAY

DARRYL *sits practically comatose in a big chair. His eyes have a dull glaze as he stares first at one wall, then another.*

INT. CAR—DAY

*A* TIGHT SHOT *of a tape being shoved into the cassette deck and Aretha Franklin singing "Save Me" at full volume.*

**END VOICE-OVER SEQUENCE**

INT. FBI JET—DAY

MAX *and* HAL *sit next to each other in the jet.* HAL *tries to appear as if he's used to all this.* MAX *holds a cellular phone to his ear.* TIGHT SHOT *of* MAX *as we hear through the phone:*

> POLICE
> (*offscreen, on phone*)
>
> . . . Abducted . . . shot up the car . . . stole the officer's
> weapon . . . tanker . . . blown up . . . terrorized . . .

MAX's face becomes troubled and more serious than we've seen so far. He looks at HAL as he hangs up the phone.

> MAX
>
> You're not even going to believe this.

EXT. FBI JET—DAY

*The jet banks off to the left.*

EXT. DESERT ROAD—DAY

**OVER MUSIC:**

*A* WIDE SHOT *of the car speeding through the desert on an empty highway.* DRIVING SHOT: *"Save Me" is still playing on the car stereo.* THELMA *has her face to the sun with her eyes closed.* LOUISE *is driving with a fierce intensity. They hardly resemble the two women that started out for a weekend in the mountains two days earlier. Although their faces are tanned and lined and their hair is blowing wildly there is a sense of serenity that pervades.*

EXT. HELIPORT—DAY

HAL *and* MAX *are climbing out of the jet and running across the tarmac to a waiting helicopter.* MAX *is carrying a walkie-talkie now.*

EXT. CAR—DAY

THELMA *sits up suddenly. She turns to look behind them.*

THELMA<br>( deadly serious )

Oh shit. Louise . . .

Louise's point of view is into the rearview mirror. An Arizona State Police car is bearing down on them really fast. The lights are flashing.

LOUISE

Is your seat belt on?

THELMA puts her seat belt on. LOUISE floors the car and it streaks off, putting some distance between them and the police car. THELMA looks back at the police car. She looks scared.

THELMA

I guess we shoulda made some kinda plan for what to
do if we get caught.

LOUISE

Yeah, right. When have we had time?

INT. ARIZONA STATE POLICE CAR—DAY

*The state* POLICEMAN *is on his radio.*

POLICEMAN

. . . requesting assistance. In pursuit of red Impala,
1966, license, Arkansas seven, one nine, william, ze-
bra, adam . . .

RADIO

Roger. Be advised (*breaks up*) armed and extremely
dangerous . . .

EXT. ARIZONA STATE POLICE HEADQUARTERS—DAY

*A steady stream of state police cars pulls out of the parking lot with lights flash-*
*ing while other policemen are running to their cars, still parked in the lot.*

INT. CAR—DAY

THELMA

How far are we from Mexico?

LOUISE

About two hundred and fifty miles.

THELMA

How long do you think that'll take?

EXT. DESERT ROAD—DAY

*There are now two police cars behind them about half a mile back. They are going really fast.*

INT. CAR—DAY

THELMA
(*looking back*)

Uh-oh. There's another one.

LOUISE and THELMA both are looking back at the two police cars following them. They turn back around just in time to see that a third Arizona State Police car has pulled into the middle of an intersection of the only road that crosses theirs for miles. They both scream. LOUISE swerves just in time to keep from hitting it broadside. She goes off the road and has to struggle to pull her car back onto the road, leaving a huge cloud of dust.

LOUISE

Shit!!

THELMA
(*indignant*)

Did you see that guy?! He was right in the middle of
the road!

EXT. DESERT ROAD—DAY

*The first two police cars are approaching the same intersection. They are driving side by side. There is still a huge cloud of dust that now covers the third car in the middle of the intersection.*

INT. POLICE CAR NO. 1—DAY

*Policeman No. 1's point of view is of a huge cloud of dust blowing across the road as he approaches the intersection. It clears to reveal the third police car in the middle of the road just as he and police car No. 2 reach the intersection.* ANGLE ON *policeman No. 1 as he screams and swerves to the right.*

INT. POLICE CAR NO. 3—DAY

ANGLE ON *policeman No. 3 as he sees both police cars heading right for him at 120 miles per hour. He screams and ducks down into the seat.*

ANOTHER ANGLE: *police car No. 1 swerves to the right. Police car No. 2 swerves to the left, both barely missing police car No. 3.*

ANOTHER ANGLE: *police car No. 1 and police car No. 2 both pull back onto the road right next to each other.*

INT. POLICE CAR NO. 3—DAY

*Policeman No. 3 sits up in the seat. He can't believe he isn't dead. He puts his car in gear and takes off down the road after them.*

INT. CAR—DAY

> LOUISE
> (*looking in rearview mirror*)

Shit!

> THELMA

What?!

> LOUISE

What?! What d'you think?!

> THELMA

Oh.

EXT. DESERT GHOST TOWN—DAY

LOUISE *and* THELMA *blow through a stand of buildings left from when the train went through here. There are two parallel streets on either side of the one they're on and as they pass by the buildings they can see police cars roaring down these parallel streets trying to "head them off at the pass."* LOUISE *floors it and her car screams ahead.*

> LOUISE
>
> We probably shoulda filled up the car before we blew up that truck.

> THELMA
>
> Why?

> LOUISE
>
> They'll probably catch us when we have to stop for gas!

> THELMA
>
> Louise . . . no matter what happens, I'm glad I came with you.

> LOUISE
>
> You're CRAZY!

> THELMA
>
> I know this whole thing is my fault. I know it is.

> LOUISE
>
> Thelma, it's not your fault!

THELMA

If we get caught, which it looks like the chances are
pretty good right now that we will, I have an idea.

LOUISE

I hope to God it's a good one.

THELMA

Let's say I did it.

LOUISE

Did what?!

THELMA

Everything. Let's say I did everything.

LOUISE

You didn't kill anybody, Thelma!

THELMA

I know, Louise, but let's just say I did. It's close enough
to the truth to stick!

LOUISE

That's the death penalty, Thelma! Have you ever
heard of the death penalty?! You think I'm gonna let
you say that?! OH, CHRIST!!!

EXT. DESERT ROAD—DAY

*Up ahead, the road is blocked by five state police cars.* LOUISE *swerves off the road and begins driving through the desert. All the police officers jump into their cars and take off across the desert after them. The police cars that were behind them drive off the road as well, and they are now being pursued by at least ten cars.*

THELMA

God! It looks like the army!

THELMA starts to laugh. LOUISE is only concerned with missing the cacti and other obstacles that lay before her.

EXT. DESERT—DAY

*It does look like an army. More police cars have joined, and from every direction police cars are swarming across the desert, although none are in front of them. Way off in the distance, a helicopter joins the chase.*

INT. CAR—DAY

THELMA *is looking way up ahead in the distance.*

THELMA

Louise!

LOUISE

What?!

THELMA

What in the hell is that up there?

LOUISE

Where?!

THELMA

Way up ahead!

LOUISE strains to see. Whatever it is, LOUISE is barreling toward it, the car leaving the ground as they fly through the desert.

LOUISE

Oh my God!!

LOUISE starts to laugh and cry at the same time.

THELMA

What in the hell is it?!

LOUISE

It's the goddamn Grand Canyon!

EXT. DESERT—DAY

*Behind them is a huge wall of dust created by all the police cars following them. In front of them, looking larger every moment, is the awesome splendor of the Grand Canyon.*

INT. CAR—DAY

THELMA
(*elated*)

Isn't it beautiful?!!

LOUISE has tears streaming down her face as she realizes there is absolutely no escape. She continues barreling toward it without slowing down. All the police cars are still following about half a mile behind. The car is bouncing and flying across the desert. Finally, they get about two hundred yards from the edge and LOUISE slams on the brakes.

THELMA

It's amazing, isn't it?

LOUISE

What is?

THELMA

How one thing . . . one little . . .

She can't think of the words.

LOUISE

. . . moment of weakness . . .

THELMA

. . . yeah . . . just one little slip . . . can just change everything.

LOUISE

We're never gonna get out of this. You know that, right? This is never gonna be over.

THELMA and LOUISE are just waiting for the cars to catch up. The police cars stop in a line about two hundred yards behind them. The dust from the cars is blowing across them. They just sit looking at the Grand Canyon. From the canyon the FBI helicopter rises up in front of the car.

INT. FBI HELICOPTER—DAY

HAL *sees* THELMA *and* LOUISE *for the first time. They are sitting in the car, oblivious, in a way, to all the activity around them. He takes his eyes off them only long enough to look at* MAX. *His eyes say, "I didn't expect them to look so human!"*

INT. CAR—DAY

> THELMA
>
> You're a good friend.

> LOUISE
>
> You too, sweetie, the best.

> THELMA
>
> I guess I went a little crazy, huh?

> LOUISE
>
> No . . . You've always been crazy. This is just the first chance you've had to really express yourself.

> THELMA
> (*serious*)
>
> I guess everything from here on in is gonna be pretty shitty.

> LOUISE
>
> Unbearable, I'd imagine.

THELMA

I guess everything we've got to lose is already gone anyway.

LOUISE

How do you stay so positive?

They smile.

INT. FBI HELICOPTER—DAY

*Hal's* POINT OF VIEW: *He sees* THELMA *and* LOUISE *facing each other. They look so nice. He can't stop looking. He borrows the binoculars from* MAX. *As they fly above the scene* HAL *sees the row of police officers surrounding* THELMA *and* LOUISE *on the ground. Some of the police sharpshooters are sporting sniper rifles.* HAL *looks to* MAX.

HAL

Hey! Don't let them shoot those girls. This is too much. They got guns pointed at 'em!

MAX

The women are armed, Hal. This is standard. Now, you stay calm here. These boys know what they're doin'.

INT. CAR—DAY

THELMA

God, I don't know if I've got the strength for this one.

> LOUISE
> (*shaking her head*)

I know I don't.

> THELMA
> (*tired*)

Then let's not.

> LOUISE

What?

> THELMA

Let's not get caught.

> LOUISE

What are you talkin' about?

> THELMA
> (*indicating the Grand Canyon*)

Go.

> LOUISE

What?

THELMA is smiling at her.

> THELMA

Go.

They look at each other, look back at the wall of police cars, and then look back at each other.

POLICE
(*over loudspeaker*)

THIS IS THE ARIZONA HIGHWAY PATROL. YOU
ARE UNDER ARREST. YOU ARE CONSIDERED
ARMED AND DANGEROUS. ANY FAILURE TO
OBEY ANY COMMAND WILL BE CONSIDERED AN
ACT OF AGGRESSION AGAINST US.

TIGHT SHOT of cartridges being loaded into automatic rifle.

SHOT of THELMA and LOUISE through the cross hairs of a gun sight.
LOUISE and THELMA are looking at each other. They are trying to smile,
but their mouths are twisted with fear.

POLICE
(*over loudspeaker*)

TURN OFF THE ENGINE AND PUT YOUR HANDS
IN THE AIR!

INT. FBI HELICOPTER—DAY

HAL *is about to crawl out of his skin! He can't believe this thing is getting out
of control.*

HAL
(*to* MAX)

Let me talk to 'em! I can't believe this!

MAX goes around HAL and continues walking. HAL jumps in front of
MAX again and blocks his way.

MAX
(*sternly*)

We are way out of your jurisdiction, now come on!
Calm down!

HAL
(*under his breath*)

Shit! I can't fucking believe this!

HAL walks along with a look of total disbelief on his face. He's shaking his head. Slowly he breaks into a trot and starts heading toward the front line.

> MAX
> (*shouting*)

Hey. Hey!

HAL is running now and clears the front line of cars. There is a lot of confusion among the officers on the front row. Some shout, some lower their guns to look.

INT. CAR—DAY

*They are still looking at each other really hard. They smile, they embrace and kiss, best friends. A B. B. King song entitled "Better Not Look Down" begins. It is very upbeat.*

> LOUISE

Are you sure?

THELMA nods.

> THELMA

Hit it.

LOUISE puts the car in gear and floors it. Cut to:

INT. FBI HELICOPTER—DAY

HAL*'s eyes widen for a moment at what he sees and then a sense of calm overtakes him and he mouths the words "all right."*

> B. B. KING SONG: *I've been around and I've seen some things*
> *People movin' faster than the speed of sound*

*Faster than a speedin' bullet.*
*People livin' like Superman, all day and all night*
*And I won't say if it's wrong or I won't say if it's right*
*I'm pretty fast myself. But I do have some advice to pass along*
*Right here in the words to this song . . .*

EXT. DESERT—DAY

*The cops all lower their weapons as looks of shock and disbelief cover their faces. A cloud of dust blows through the frame as the speeding car sails over the edge of the cliff.*

B.B. KING SONG: *Better not look down, if you wanna keep on flyin'*
*Put the hammer down, keep it full speed ahead*
*Better not look back or you might just wind up cryin'.*
*You can keep it movin' if you don't look down . . .*

**FADE TO WHITE . . .**

# *Something to Talk About*

## Cast

| | |
|---|---|
| Grace Bichon | Julia Roberts |
| Eddie Bichon | Dennis Quaid |
| Caroline Bichon | Haley Aull |
| Wyly King | Robert Duvall |
| Georgia King | Gena Rowlands |
| Emma Rae | Kyra Sedgwick |
| Jamie Johnson | Brett Cullen |
| Hank Corrigan | Muse Watson |
| Aunt Rae | Anne Shropshire |
| Eula | Ginnie Randall |
| Dr. Frank Lewis | Terrence P. Currier |
| Mrs. Pinkerton | Mary Nell Santacroce |
| Barbaranelle | Rebecca Koon |
| Edna | Rhoda Griffis |
| Jessie Gaines | Shannon Eubanks |
| Kitty | Lisa Roberts |
| Lorene Tuttle | Deborah Hobart |
| Lucy | Amy Parrish |
| Mary Jane | Helen Baldwin |
| Nadine | Libby Whittemore |
| Norma Leggett | Punky Leonard |
| Anne | Jayme Price |
| Sonny | Michael Flippo |
| Frank | Beau Holden |
| June | Sandra Thigpen |
| Dub | Bennie Jenkins |
| Harry | Rusty Hendrickson |
| Announcer | J. Don Ferguson |

# Filmmakers

| | |
|---|---|
| Writer | Callie Khouri |
| Director | Lasse Hallstrom |
| Producer | Paula Weinstein |
| Producer | Anthea Sylbert |
| Director of Photography | Sven Nykvist |
| Editor | Mia Goldman, A.C.E. |
| Production Designer | Mel Bourne |
| Music | Hans Zimmer |
| Casting | Marion Dougherty |

INT. BEDROOM—MORNING

*Hands dive into a pile of wild hair and begin French-braiding it. Reveal in a mirror* GRACE KING BICHON, *dressed in a T-shirt that used to be white, riding pants and boots. She's wearing pearls and looks like a cross between a grown debutante and a stable hand, which is exactly what she is. She is a perfectionist who always falls short of her own expectations.*

> EDDIE
>
> So, what have you got on the docket for today?

GRACE *screams, startled out of her wits as her husband,* EDDIE BICHON, *steps into the mirror's reflection to tie his tie. He's a Southern frat boy, all grown up, or as grown up as they ever get. And he's incredibly handsome, a real looker.*

| GRACE | EDDIE |
|---|---|
| Aaiiee!! Goddamn, Eddie, will you make some noise or something! | Grace! Cut that out! Jesus Christ you're gonna give me a heart attack! |

They calm down and resume their tasks.

> GRACE
>
> I've got to go out to the barn. Daddy wants to have some kind of a meeting with me and Hank about the Grand Prix.

> EDDIE
>
> What about?

GRACE

He just likes to start grinding us every year about this
time. Makes him feel in control.

EDDIE

Where's doodlebug?

GRACE

She better be getting dressed. (*Shouting.*) Caroline,
what are you doing?

CAROLINE, their eight-year-old, a miniature of GRACE, comes bounding
into the room.

CAROLINE

Getting ready! Am I gonna ride?

GRACE

If we have time!

EDDIE

Hey doodlebug! Where've you been all night?!

CAROLINE
(*laughing*)

Sleeping!

EDDIE

What'd you dream about?

CAROLINE

What do you think?

He laughs and kisses her. She runs out.

GRACE
(*to* EDDIE)

Hey, I've got to take her to Pinkerton's today to get fitted for her riding suit. You want to meet us there and then we can take her to lunch.

EDDIE

I can't do lunch. I've got a meeting I can't get out of. Wanna meet before?

GRACE

Can't. Gotta Charity League meeting. They stuck me with chairman of the cookbook committee.

EDDIE

How 'bout tomorrow.

GRACE

Tomorrow's Saturday.

EDDIE

Gotta golf game. How's Monday?

GRACE

If I can stave her off that long.

EDDIE

Okay. Call June and have her schedule it. Are you gonna cook tonight?

GRACE

Depends. Are you gonna be here?

EDDIE

I'll call ya.

GRACE

O.K.

EXT. GRACE AND EDDIE'S HOUSE—MORNING

GRACE *and* EDDIE *step out onto the porch of their beautiful old two-story Georgian house that's been restored and redecorated by* GRACE. *They kiss on the cheek and trot down the steps to their respective cars, his a Mercedes, hers a Jeep Grand Cherokee. They both get in and start to drive down the driveway.* GRACE *slams on the brakes and backs up to the front of the house. She gets out of the car, trots back up the steps and unlocks the front door.* CAROLINE *marches out to the car indignantly.*

EXT. KING HOUSE DRIVEWAY—MORNING

*A* CLOSE SHOT *of a sign with a silhouette of a hunter jumper that reads* KING FARMS *and, in smaller letters underneath,* WYLY KING—OWNER; *in even smaller letters underneath that, it says* HANK CORRIGAN—TRAINER.

EXT. KING HOUSE DRIVEWAY—MORNING

GRACE'S *Jeep turns past the King Farms sign, into a long tree-lined driveway that leads up to the barn and the big house.*

INT. KING FARMS TRAINING BARN—MORNING

GRACE *and* CAROLINE *come into a busy training barn.* GRACE *addresses some of the men working there as she passes.*

GRACE

Hey, Dub.

DUB

Morning, Grace.

GRACE

Harry, take the trailer over to the Macks's to pick up
Joe's Whimsy around four-thirty. Sheila'll ride over
here with you and help get him squared away.

HARRY

Yes ma'am.

GRACE

Tell Hank before you go, so he can be here.

HARRY

No problem.

GRACE goes into her office. CAROLINE is standing on a mounting step at
a stall door, plying a horse with carrots. A plaque on the door says
SILVER BELLS. She strokes his face and coos to him, calling him by his
stable name, Possum, for his silvery gray color and pink nose, while
he lips her pockets. Both CAROLINE and Possum look as the big door
at the end of the barn slides open.

WYLY KING, a man in his sixty-fifth year of heart-stopping hand-
someness—aged to perfection, he says—with flowing white hair and
a Darth Vader stride, comes down the breezeway toward his granddaughter. His blue eyes crinkle in a smile that always comes when he
sees this little girl.

WYLY

Caught ya! You tryin' to bribe ol' Possum?

CAROLINE

Hey, Gramps.

WYLY

Miss Lily's gonna get jealous and dump you off in the ring. You gotta save the treats for the horse you're gonna ride.

Standing on the step she is almost the same height as WYLY. She suddenly turns to face him, grabbing his vest.

CAROLINE

Gramps! Why?! Please let me! I don't want to ride a pony! I want to ride a horse! There's kids younger than me already.

WYLY

Now honey, hold on a minute. First of all, you can *win* on Miss Lily . . . and you're gonna win on Miss Lily . . .

He picks her up from the step and starts to walk with her legs wrapped around his waist, but she's heavy!

WYLY
(*straining*)

Oh good Lord, let me put you down.

CAROLINE squeezes him tighter with her legs. He winces slightly but she refuses to let go.

CAROLINE

See? See how strong my legs are?

WYLY

Honey I gotta put you down! Have mercy on an old man.

She lets go and drops to the floor as WYLY quickly recovers his composure.

WYLY

And second, he's too damn big for you. You've gotta learn to recognize your limitations . . .

CAROLINE
(*interrupting*)

How old was Mama when she won on Sunny Girl?

WYLY

*Nine.*

CAROLINE
(*skeptically*)

How much did she weigh?

WYLY

Honey, I don't remember, now don't get yourself all worked up! You're gonna have to take this up with your mama, have you done that?

CAROLINE

Yes.

WYLY

And?

CAROLINE

You think I'd be down here beggin' you if she'd said
yes?! Just put me on that horse and I'll win the junior
championship! And how come everybody thinks they
gotta tell me when I'm ready. I tell *you* when I'm ready!
And I'm READY! And I'm about runnin' out of pa-
tience with you people!

She's in the middle of a full-blown tirade now. DUB, an old stable hand
who's come to see what all the fuss is about, trades a look of amused
astonishment with WYLY. CAROLINE realizes what she's saying and stops
cold.

WYLY

Who's that remind you of?

DUB

It's uncanny.

WYLY

Now go give DUB a hand and earn your keep around
here. I gotta talk to your mama now.

CAROLINE starts to run.

WYLY

Hey! Come back here and kiss your Grampa. I oughta
swat you one for carryin' on this way.

He pretends he's going to, but sweeps her up, kisses her and lets her go. HANK CORRIGAN, a weathered man in his early forties, the horse trainer for King Farms, comes riding into the barn, stops and hops off the horse. DUB comes over and takes the reins and leads the horse to the grooming area.

WYLY

Hey, Hank! How'sit goin'?

HANK

Good. Great.

WYLY

Good! Grace needs to see you.

HANK

Now?

WYLY

In a bit. I've gotta talk to her for a minute. After that.

HANK

Yes sir.

WYLY disappears into the office.

INT. TRAINING BARN—GRACE'S OFFICE—MORNING

WYLY *walks in on* GRACE, *who sits behind her desk.*

GRACE
(*startled*)

Hi Daddy.

These two are always slightly perturbed at the sight of each other, and they see each other every day. She manages the training barn and handles the business side of the horse training. WYLY shuts the door behind him and gets to business.

WYLY

All right. Have a Heart went on the market last week.

GRACE

Yeah?

WYLY

The one from California, Jamie Johnson's horse. He won the Hampton Classic in September.

GRACE

I know the horse. How much is he askin'?

WYLY

One hundred and fifty thousand.

GRACE

That's all? What's wrong with him?

WYLY

Well, nothing. Johnson's having to sell 'cause of his divorce. Anyway, I bought him.

GRACE is stunned.

> GRACE
>
> You did *what*?!

> WYLY
>
> I've just got a feeling about him. I think this is his year.
> He's got Grand Prix Champion written all over him.
> And . . . I'm gonna ride him.

GRACE stands up, in shock.

> GRACE
>
> But, Daddy, without even discussing it with us?!

> WYLY
>
> There's nothing to discuss.

He knows he's dropped a bombshell. He's had a lot of experience at
this kind of thing and he lets it sink in.

> GRACE
> (*shaken*)
>
> Jesus H. Christ, Daddy! What are you talking about?
> What about Ransom? Hank's gonna . . .

Just then the office door opens and CAROLINE starts to come in.

> CAROLINE
>
> Mom? Dub said I could . . .

GRACE pushes the door closed.

GRACE

Not now, honey!!

WYLY

Ransom's . . . not ready. I don't have the same feelin'
about him.

GRACE

What have the last five years been about? He's had a
great year.

WYLY

That's enough! Now I've been doin' this since you
were tapping on a high chair with a teaspoon! I'm
doin' what I'm doin'!

GRACE tries to reason with him.

GRACE

Daddy, Hank doesn't have time to take on another
horse this close to the show!

WYLY

He doesn't have to. Jamie Johnson is bringing him
himself. He's gonna work with him until after the
show. That was part of the deal. He's coming tomorrow with the horse, and the rest of his barn is coming

out in two weeks. Fourteen all together. Have Dub hire
as many extra grooms as it's gonna take.

GRACE

So, you're gonna ride against Hank and Ransom?

WYLY

No. We're not gonna enter Ransom. Not this year. He
can wait another year.

There is an appalling silence.

GRACE

But that doesn't make any sense!

WYLY

Honey, when this is your place, you can do whatever
you want.

GRACE

Daddy . . . Hank'll quit.

WYLY

Well, honey, here's a good opportunity for you to uti-
lize your people skills . . . so you see to it that he
doesn't. You hear me? You understand?

GRACE

You can't do this. It's not fair!

WYLY

It's done. Now roll with it.

He walks out of the office, closing the door behind him. She convulses with sheer frustration:

GRACE
(*quietly*)

Goddamn sonofafuckingbitch! Shit! Shit! Shit!

WYLY sticks his head back in the door.

WYLY

You watch that mouth now.

INT. TRAINING BARN—MORNING

HANK *is over near the grooming area.* WYLY *heads out of the barn.*

WYLY
(*cheerfully*)

Hey Hank. She can see you now.

CUT TO: GRACE and HANK are charging down the breezeway, in the direction of GRACE's car.

HANK
(*stunned and angry*)

Well then goddamnit, I quit! I don't need this shit!

GRACE

Hank, wait!

HANK

I wish the sonofabitch would die in a fiery car crash!

GRACE
(*bitterly agreeing*)

I know, Hank. Get in line. But just listen . . .

HANK
(*furious*)

No! You listen! I'm not gonna just sit by while the
sonofabitch ruins my career! This is Ransom's year!
This is it! I know like I know my own . . . Well, he can
kiss my ass!

GRACE

Hank, please! Give me some time! Maybe I can make
him see reason!

HANK

Like hell.

GRACE

You can't do this to me!

Her younger sister, EMMA RAE KING, pulls up. EMMA RAE's looks make
GRACE seem tame in comparison. She got her father's determination
and her mother's tenacity and that's why she runs the family estate
auction and real estate business. And she doesn't suffer fools gladly.

EMMA RAE

Grace! Is Daddy in there?

GRACE

No!

GRACE hops into her car.

EMMA RAE

Grace, hold on a sec!

GRACE

I can't! I've got a Charity League meeting! Did you
know about this, Emma Rae?!

EMMA RAE

What? About this horse thing?

GRACE

Thanks a lot for tellin' me!

EMMA RAE

Hey! Check your machine, Grace!

GRACE starts her car and backs out.

EMMA RAE

Grace! WAIT!

GRACE doesn't. She blows down the long driveway and stops when she
gets to the road.

INT. GRACE'S JEEP—MORNING

*She hears* EMMA RAE *'s horn blowing and looks into her rearview mirror.* CLOSE UP *on mirror:* EMMA RAE *'s car is right behind her and* EMMA RAE *is waving out the window. The passenger-side door of* EMMA RAE*'s car opens and* CAROLINE *hops out and runs up.*

    CLOSE-UP *on* GRACE *as she realizes she's forgotten her daughter once more. She rubs her forehead with her fingers.*

GRACE
(under her breath)

Oh God. Help me.

EXT. CHARITY LEAGUE HOUSE—DAY

*In the front yard of a quaint old two-story house is an old but elegantly carved wood sign that reads:* CHARITY LEAGUE—ESTABLISHED 1893.

NORMA
(voice-over; a real southern accent)

. . . and a great big thanks for Jessie Gaines and her husband, Happy, for the absolutely beautiful job they did repainting the children's ward! The stenciling is absolutely wonderful!

INT. CHARITY LEAGUE HOUSE—DAY

*All the women clap and look at a beaming red* JESSIE GAINES. *The large wood-paneled room is full of women of all ages, sitting in chairs all facing a panel of eight women at the front of the room. We watch* GRACE, *who is still in her riding clothes and looks out of place. She plays with her pearls, putting them in her mouth. She tries hard to pay attention.*

NORMA

Now, to the business of the centennial cookbook. I know we all want this to be our best ever, so I'll ask our committee chairman to bring us up to date. Grace?

GRACE
(*caught unaware*)

Well, the deadline for recipe submissions is December second and it would help if they were typed.

A groan from the gallery.

GRACE

Also if you want to substitute vegetable shortening wherever it says bacon grease or lard, you might want to think about that. Nell McGeehee asked me to mention that because her husband, Bobby, is recovering from a triple-bypass right now. Also Lucy is taking over for me until after the Grand Prix. I'm up to my neck in horses till then, and I think that's it.

She looks at LUCY, her best friend at the Charity League, for confirmation.

LUCY

Names.

GRACE

What?

LUCY

Names!

GRACE

Oh right. Well . . . the committee thinks . . . we've looked at a lot of other cookbooks . . . and we've always been listed with our married names underneath

the recipe . . . and frankly the practice of excluding
our first names . . . it looks outdated. We want to just
list our names, first, middle and last. That's all.

A smattering of applause mixed with some uneasy glances, then
silence.

MARY JANE

Does this have something to do with Hillary?

EDNA

I always thought the way it was looked quaint.

A spontaneous and *overlapping* "discussion" erupts. And it sounds like
a room full of blue jays.

NADINE

It doesn't look quaint, Edna, it looks antiquated! I
don't see why Harry's name should be in a cookbook.
He'd no more lift a finger to cook than to poke himself in the eye with a sharp stick.

KITTY

But what about the tradition?

LUCY

Why carry on a tradition if it's stupid and insulting?
I've got a name and I want it in the goddamn cookbook!

An older woman, with too much jewelry, too much makeup and
maybe a little too much to drink this morning, stands up.

BARBARANELLE
(*a little too loudly*)

What I'd like to know is if my name isn't in there, Mrs.
Franklin J. Caldwell the third, how the hell is anybody
gonna know who I am? I mean Barbaranelle Caldwell,
who's that? It could be his daughter for heaven's sake.

She sits.

LORENE

You wish.

BARBARANELLE

Shut up, Lorene.

NORMA

Well now, let's all calm down. This isn't something
that's going to be decided today. If there's no further
business then this meeting is adjourned.

All the women stand to leave, but the discussion continues.

BARBARANELLE

Hell, I'm proud to use my husband's name. I consider
the fact that I'm still married to the old goat one of
my greatest accomplishments.

GRACE and LUCY look at each other, baffled.

INT. HALLWAY—CHARITY LEAGUE HOUSE—DAY

*As the meeting adjourns a group of women have gathered at the back of the
room. As* GRACE *heads out,* LUCY, *who is part of the huddle, motions her over.*

*They are all looking at* EDNA*'s wrist, which is sporting a diamond and sapphire tennis bracelet. They are all kidding her as they admire it.*

BARBARANELLE

Lord have mercy. Either you've been really good or he's been really bad . . .

LORENE

That is some major guilt there . . .

MARY JANE

He bought it from Calhoun. Want me to find out how much it cost?

EDNA

I tell you, the bigger a rascal he is, the better the birthday present.

GRACE and LUCY walk away from the group.

LUCY
(*wryly to* GRACE)

Well if that's the way it works, that puts us in the running for the Hope diamond.

GRACE

Speak for yourself.

INT. KIDS' ROOM—CHARITY LEAGUE HOUSE—DAY

*All the mothers are collecting their kids.* AUNT RAE, GRACE*'s great-aunt, comes over to* GRACE, *with* CAROLINE *in tow. She is seventy-five years young and she is a real live wire.*

GRACE

Hey, Aunt Rae, I didn't see you when we came in! How are you? ..

AUNT RAE
(*smiling*)

Oh, fine as can be. You know, your mother called. She wants to change the menu for the Grand Prix party.

GRACE

What for? Everybody loves it.

AUNT RAE

She wants shrimp. She said she's just sick to death of ham and barbecue. They've been doin' it that way for thirty-five years, I don't know why it suddenly bothers her now. Bring this little precious thing over to my house and let me give her some lunch . . .

CAROLINE
(*apprehensively*)

Mom.

GRACE

I've got to take her down to Pinkerton's to get her fitted for her riding habit. I promised.

AUNT RAE

Well that's wonderful! Who're you gonna ride?

|  GRACE  |  CAROLINE  |
| --- | --- |
| Miss Lily. | Possum. |

GRACE

No you're not, young lady. We've been through this
a thousand and one times!

CAROLINE
(*exasperated*)

Is this because I don't have all my teeth?

GRACE

We're not going to discuss this . . .

CAROLINE
(*plaintively*)

But why . . .

GRACE

No! We better get going. I hate to fight with my child
in public.

AUNT RAE gives CAROLINE a hug and whispers in her ear:

AUNT RAE

You gotta wear them down.

Then she hugs GRACE.

EXT. DOWNTOWN—DAY

EDDIE *strolls up to the entrance of a mirrored skyscraper, but does not go in.
He looks around and checks his watch. He checks out his reflection in the building and straightens his tie.*

EXT. DOWNTOWN STREET—DAY

GRACE *and* CAROLINE *are driving slowly down the street. On the corner is the mirrored skyscraper.*

INT. GRACE'S JEEP—DAY

GRACE *and* CAROLINE *are in the car.*

> GRACE
>
> Keep your eyes peeled for a parking spot, sweetie plum.

> CAROLINE
>
> Yuck. That's gross, mom.

> GRACE
>
> I know, but Gram used to say it to me and now it's a habit. She'd also say "I'll keep an eye out for you."

> CAROLINE
>
> Gross.

They stop at the stoplight at the corner, in front of the mirrored building.

> CAROLINE
>
> Why do buildings have stories?

> GRACE
>
> What do you mean? Don't pick your nose, honey.

CAROLINE

Why do they say it's twenty stories or fifty stories high?

GRACE

That's a good question. I'm not sure why that is. We're gonna have to look that one up.

GRACE looks out her window. She sees EDDIE. He's got his back to her but she can tell it's him.

EXT. DOWNTOWN—DAY

*A young woman in a red crepe suit comes out of the revolving door of the mirrored skyscraper and walks up behind* EDDIE *and gives him a little tug on the ear. He turns around and smiles. They kiss. He puts his arms around her waist and pulls her to him. He whispers something.* GRACE *sees the woman's arm slide around his shoulders. She strains to focus. Then she realizes* CAROLINE *might see. She points to the street sign on the other side of the street.*

GRACE
(*shakily*)

What's that sign say, ladybug? Can you read what that says?

She looks back and now EDDIE and the woman are walking along, look-ing very comfortable together. She watches as EDDIE and the woman kiss again.

CAROLINE
(*sounding it out*)

Un . . . Un . . . I . . . on. Onion. Onion Street.

GRACE'S POINT OF VIEW is of EDDIE and the young woman coming to some kind of agreement and heading into the parking structure.

                    GRACE
                  (*quietly*)

   No, honey. Union. That's Union. Street.

GRACE is staring, even after they've gone, the color completely gone
from her face. She looks like she's been punched in the stomach.

                   CAROLINE

   Mom, green means go.

A car honks behind her and GRACE lurches forward.

                   CAROLINE
                  (*repeating*)

   Union.

INT. PINKERTON'S EQUESTRIAN SHOP—DAY

GRACE *stands, pretending to be looking at riding jackets, hiding her face, try-*
*ing not to cry.*

INT. EQUESTRIAN SHOP—UPSTAIRS FITTING ROOM—DAY

CAROLINE *stands, looking at herself in the three-way mirror. She wears a beau-*
*tiful riding habit and at this moment looks like a grown woman trapped in*
*the body of a child. An ancient, doting* MRS. PINKERTON *pins the hem of her*
*pants.*

                MRS. PINKERTON
               (*calling to* GRACE)

   Honey, come look at this and see if this is all right.

GRACE gets a hold of herself and goes to look at CAROLINE. It takes her
breath away.

MRS. PINKERTON

That must take you back.

GRACE and CAROLINE look at each other for a long moment.

CAROLINE

Please can I get the boots?

GRACE

Honey, they're so expensive and your little feet are gonna grow so much!

CAROLINE

But why spend all that money on the suit and then chintz out on the boots?!

GRACE

Uuhh . . . Can I use your phone?

MRS. PINKERTON

In the office, there.

CAROLINE

Why do we always have to call Daddy when we want to buy something?

GRACE hurls herself into the office.

MRS. PINKERTON

You should have seen your mama and your Aunt Emma Rae when they were your age.

CAROLINE

Did they get to ride whoever they wanted?

MRS. PINKERTON

Oh yes, your grandaddy would put them up on any big ol' thing and they would just ride their little hearts out.

INT. EQUESTRIAN SHOP OFFICE—DAY

*The walls are covered with photos of horses and riders. There is even a picture of* GRACE *and* EMMA RAE *as little girls, holding the reins of their horses.* GRACE *stares at this picture as she picks up the phone and dials a number. A* RECEPTIONIST *answers the phone.*

RECEPTIONIST
(*offscreen, on phone*)

Bichon Partners.

GRACE

Eddie Bichon's office please.

INT. EDDIE BICHON'S OFFICE—DAY

EDDIE'*s secretary answers the phone.*

JUNE

Edward Bichon's office.

GRACE
(*offscreen, on phone, shakily*)

Hello, June. It's Grace. Can I speak to Eddie?

JUNE
(*pleasantly*)

Miz Bichon, he's not in. He said he'd be at a meeting for the rest of the afternoon.

INT. EQUESTRIAN SHOP OFFICE—DAY

GRACE *struggles to sound offhand and casual.*

GRACE

Did he say where?

JUNE
(*offscreen, on phone*)

No ma'am, he sure didn't. If he calls in you want me to have him call you?

GRACE

No.

She hangs up.

INT. GRACE'S KITCHEN—EVENING

CAROLINE *sits at the kitchen table, eating her dinner.* GRACE's *plate sits untouched while* GRACE *stands at the counter, quietly playing back messages on the answering machine.*

ANSWERING MACHINE

. . . need help testing recipes for the cookbook. Besides I've gained ten pounds. (*Fast forward,* EMMA RAE's *voice:*) . . . some kind of deal, the guy was asking five, but the horse is being sold as part of a divorce settlement so Dad's got him down to the high twos. What can I say, Grace, Daddy's an asshole, big surprise. I'll call you if I find out anything else.

She holds the fast-forward button down, then:

ANSWERING MACHINE
(EDDIE'S *voice*)

. . . Dad wants me to go out to dinner with these clients so I'll be home by eleven o'clock. Kiss the doodlebug for me. Bye.

She rewinds to the beginning of the message.

ANSWERING MACHINE

Hey, Grace. It's me. This meeting took longer than we thought and now Dad wants me . . .

She rewinds the entire tape. She looks over her shoulder at CAROLINE, who sits playing with her food and talking quietly to herself.

INT. GRACE'S BEDROOM—NIGHT

GRACE *is in bed.* CAROLINE *lies sleeping next to her, in her nightie and new riding boots.* GRACE *agitatedly flips through a magazine without looking at the pages. She looks at the clock that reads 10:59. As it flips to 11:00,* GRACE *leaps out of bed. She doesn't know what to do, but she's going crazy waiting.*

INT. GRACE'S JEEP—NIGHT

GRACE *and* CAROLINE *are in the car, both in their nightgowns.* GRACE *is cruising slowly down a street looking for* EDDIE*'s car, which she spots and so does* CAROLINE.

CAROLINE

Hey, that's Daddy's car.

GRACE rolls up in front of a bar, with a big picture window. She strains to see inside, but the glare off the window from the streetlights makes it difficult. She double-parks, puts the flashers on and hops out.

GRACE

Wait here, sweetie.

She walks up to the window and looks inside. GRACE's point of view is of EDDIE sitting next to the woman from downtown, at a crowded table of his friends and some women who either look remarkably good for their age or are still in college.

INT. BAR—NIGHT

*The patrons start to notice* GRACE *and* CAROLINE, *who has gotten out of the car, standing outside in their pajamas.* GRACE *knocks on the window.*

GRACE
(*from outside*)

Eddie! I can see you!

EXT. BAR—NIGHT

CAROLINE *thinks this is great and begins to knock too.*

CAROLINE

Hi, Daddy! Hi!

GRACE

Ladybug! Get back in the car!

INT. BAR—NIGHT

*Everyone in the place is looking at the window.* EDDIE *suddenly realizes that the nutty woman outside is his wife. So do the other people at the table.*

SONNY

Uh-oh. You're busted, buddy.

EDDIE stands, completely panicked.

GRACE
(*from outside*)

Get your ASS OUT HERE NOW!

EDDIE

Jesus H. Christ!

FRANK

Yep. He was crucified too.

Everyone's really enjoying this. EDDIE scrambles out the door.

EXT. BAR—NIGHT

EDDIE *rushes out the door to* GRACE.

EDDIE

Grace?! What?! . . . Is that your nightgown?!

GRACE has picked up CAROLINE.

CAROLINE
(*happily*)

Hi, Daddy! We came to get you.

EDDIE
(*distractedly gives her a kiss*)

Hey tadpole. Let me put you in the car.

Which he does. He puts her in the backseat.

EDDIE

Now Grace, get in the car!

GRACE

No.

EDDIE

You are making a spectacle of yourself! Now get in!

He starts trying to pull her around to the driver's side. She jerks free.

GRACE

No! No! *You're* making a spectacle of me!

EDDIE

What in the hell is wrong with you!?

GRACE
(*coldly*)

I saw you.

EDDIE

What are you talking about?!

EDDIE just wants her off the street so bad he doesn't realize what she's saying. They are standing in front of the car, illuminated by the head-lights. GRACE speaks urgently, but quietly, so CAROLINE won't hear.

GRACE

I saw you. On the corner of Fifth and Union. You know what I'm talking about. I saw you. With a girl in a red crepe suit. That girl that's in there.

EDDIE does the only thing he knows how to do.

EDDIE
(*calmly*)

Honey, I don't know what you saw, but it wasn't me.

GRACE

You mean that's it? That's all I get? You're just gonna stand here and lie to me in the middle of the street? . . .

He just stares at her, knowing he's caught, not knowing what to say.

EDDIE

What? What do you want me to say?

GRACE goes suddenly calm.

GRACE

I want you to say good-bye to Caroline.

She starts to walk to the driver's side.

> EDDIE

Where're you goin'?

GRACE doesn't answer.

> EDDIE

Home to Daddy?

She stops and walks back around to the front of the car.

> GRACE
> (*deliberately, with true loathing*)

Fuck you, Eddie.

EDDIE notices that people are just standing in the window watching them like they're on television. So does GRACE and she flips them a big fat bird. She walks around and gets in the car. CAROLINE has clambered into the front seat. She's scared.

INT. JEEP—NIGHT

CAROLINE *looks to her mother.* GRACE *rolls* CAROLINE'*s window down.* EDDIE *is standing there.*

> GRACE

Kiss Daddy good-bye, angel.

She does and EDDIE leans in and gives her a big hug. One thing is true. He loves his little girl.

> EDDIE

I'll see you later, alligator.

CAROLINE
(*shaken*)

After a while, alliga . . . I mean crocodile.

GRACE starts the car and drives away.

CAROLINE

Mama? Is Daddy in trouble?

GRACE

Yes baby. He is. Daddy is in very big trouble.

She holds CAROLINE's hand as she drives away.

INT. JEEP—NIGHT

GRACE's POINT OF VIEW *of the road and the King Farms sign, lit up at night by the headlights. As* GRACE *turns into the driveway, she turns her headlights off. The lights are all on at the barn, but* GRACE *drives past, goes behind the main house and stops in front of a converted carriage house, where* EMMA RAE *lives.* EMMA RAE *looks out the window and sees* GRACE. *Her front door opens and* EMMA RAE *and her big yellow dog, Hoover, come out.* EMMA RAE *steps to the car.* GRACE *signals for her to be quiet.* CAROLINE *is sound asleep.*

INT. WYLY AND GEORGIA'S BEDROOM—NIGHT

WYLY KING *stands in the dark room watching his daughters through his bedroom window.* GEORGIA, *his wife, comes up behind him and slips her arms around him. He moves her in front of him so she has his view. She sees* GRACE *lift* CAROLINE *from the front seat.*

GEORGIA
(*under her breath*)

Oh Lord.

They watch the women and the dog go inside.

INT. EMMA RAE'S HOUSE—NIGHT

As CAROLINE sleeps in the other room, EMMA RAE and her overwrought sister whisper emphatically.

> EMMA RAE
>
> Well this is just an unholy mess. And the timing . . . right in the middle of this Wheeler Farm deal with Eddie and his dad . . . If you're expecting any loyalty from Daddy right now . . .

> GRACE
> (*bitterly*)
>
> I'm not! Believe me! I'm not completely deluded. Besides . . . it wasn't a business decision, Emma Rae! I mean I *saw* the son of a bitch!

> EMMA RAE
>
> Well Grace . . . what a fucking news flash! I've always worried about something like this happening.

> GRACE
>
> Really?! Well if you were so goddamn worried, why in the hell didn't you say something?!

> EMMA RAE
>
> What am I supposed to say? You marry a guy whose nickname in college is Hound Dog, what'd you think was gonna happen?!

GRACE

Emma Rae! Do you always have to be so goddamn sensitive?! You don't think I feel like an idiot?! I mean, I'm out there in the goddamn street . . . What am I supposed to do? Look at me! Jesus. I mean . . . What?

EMMA RAE

No, you did the right thing. You did. I'm proud of you.

EMMA RAE goes over to GRACE and gives her a hug. GRACE struggles but holds it together.

EMMA RAE

And I'm gonna kill the son of a bitch.

INT. TRUCK CAB—DAWN

*The* POINT OF VIEW *from inside the cab is of a very cushy pickup truck. k. d. lang sings as we drive down a rural road. The hands on the steering wheel take a right turn into the long driveway, passing the big King Farms sign.*

*Silhouette against the dawn sky of the pickup truck and trailer rolling up the driveway toward the house and barn.*

*Silhouette of* WYLY, HANK *and* DUB *as the truck glides to a halt in front of the barn. The driver's-side door opens and* JAMIE JOHNSON, *late thirties, steps out of the truck.* CLOSE-UP *of* CAROLINE *'s new boots crunching down the driveway to join the men.*

*Silhouette of the horse Have a Heart, hereafter known as Harvey, as* JAMIE, *his trainer, walks him in a small circle in front of* CAROLINE *and the guys. The horse wears a blanket and all the rest of the usual accoutrements. Even so, in the dim light of dawn, from far away, it is clear that this horse is magnificent.* JAMIE *is tall and handsome and goes with the horse.*

INT. EMMA RAE'S HOUSE—MORNING

*Through the window,* EMMA RAE *notices* CAROLINE, *who is still dressed in her nightgown and riding boots, talking with* WYLY. EMMA RAE *'s point of view is of* CAROLINE *flipping a bird, with* GRACE*'s exact expression, demonstrating last night's events for* WYLY.

> EMMA RAE
>
> Grace, you better get it together, Daddy's gonna be here in about ten seconds.

INT. EMMA RAE'S BEDROOM—MORNING

GRACE *leaps out of bed.*

> GRACE
>
> Oh shit!

INT. EMMA RAE'S HOUSE—MORNING

EMMA RAE*'s* POINT OF VIEW *is of* CAROLINE *running off to the big house.* WYLY *comes toward her front door. He raps twice and comes in.*

> EMMA RAE
> (*all business*)
>
> Hey Daddy, here's your schedule. The Troutman auction is at noon. I'm meeting Mr. Yopp about the financing at four, so don't be late . . .

He looks around for GRACE, *and seeing she's not in the room, asks*
EMMA RAE:

> WYLY
> (*quietly*)
>
> What in the Sam Hell is going on here?

EMMA RAE
(*innocently*)

What're you talkin' about?

WYLY

Honey, if you want to succeed in business you're gonna have to learn to lie a whole lot better than that.

GRACE comes into the room with a cheerful expression smashed onto her face like a pie.

GRACE

Hey, Daddy.

He gives EMMA RAE a look that says scram.

EMMA RAE
(*reluctantly*)

I'm gonna go see . . . 'bout . . . some stuff.

She exits, leaving GRACE and WYLY alone. WYLY starts in.

WYLY

In your goddamn nightgown? Is that part true?

GRACE

Daddy . . .

WYLY

Is that how you behave in front of your child? What in the name of God has gotten into you?

GRACE

Daddy, please . . .

WYLY

You think you're invisible?

GRACE

We're having some problems . . .

WYLY

We? Who we? He wasn't in his goddamn underwear
was he?

GRACE

No . . . I meant . . .

WYLY

How the hell is you running around town nekked
gonna solve anything? You trying to humiliate your
whole goddamn family? Do you know what your
mother is gonna say?

INT. KING HOUSE KITCHEN—MORNING

EMMA RAE *is in the kitchen along with* EULA, *the housekeeper, and* GEORGIA
LOVE KING, *a regal kind of beauty. The three of them stand staring out the
kitchen window at* EMMA RAE*'s house, as if staring at a TV. They talk quietly
as* CAROLINE *tools in and out of the kitchen, setting the table in the dining
room.*

GEORGIA
(*shaking her head*)

Oh my God. Her heart must be in a million little pieces.

EMMA RAE
(*impatiently*)

No, her pride. Now for god's sake don't get maudlin.

GEORGIA

It's just too awful! I can't *believe* he would do that! What was he thinking of?

EMMA RAE

Probably the same thing he was thinking with.

A moment passes as GEORGIA gets it.

GEORGIA
(*wearily*)

Emma Rae.

They all suddenly pretend to be occupied while CAROLINE picks up some utensils.

CAROLINE

Spoons on the right or the left?

EVERYBODY

On the right.

She leaves.

GEORGIA

And for Grace to humiliate herself like that! I just can't stand the thought of it. What in the world are we gonna do now?

EMMA RAE

Whatever it is, I'm sure it will be hopelessly ineffective.

EULA

Miss Smart.

EMMA RAE

Well, I'm going back over there. She's probably had all she can take.

GEORGIA
(*to herself*)

Oh God. Here we go.

EXT. DRIVEWAY BETWEEN BIG HOUSE AND EMMA RAE'S—MORNING

EMMA RAE *is coming out of the kitchen door at the same time* WYLY *is leaving her house. They walk toward each other without really looking like they're going to stop when they pass, but they do. When they talk, they don't look at each other. They look at the ground or past each other.*

EMMA RAE

You get her all squared away?

WYLY

She'll be all right.

                    EMMA RAE

She say what was goin' on?

                    WYLY

Just a fight.

                    EMMA RAE

Eddie's fucking somebody else.

Now they make eye contact, but only briefly.

                    WYLY

That for sure?

                    EMMA RAE

Yup.

                    WYLY

O.K. See you at noon.

INT. TRAINING BARN—GRACE'S OFFICE—DAY

GRACE *sits with her head in her hands. The phone rings and* GRACE *hits the speakerphone button. She holds her head for the whole conversation.*

                    GRACE

King Farms.

                    LUCY

Grace, it's Luce. I'm trying to make this damn hazel-nut buttercream and it looks weird.

GRACE

Like what?

LUCY

Like grainy and like it's gonna separate.

GRACE

It said "cream softened butter and sugar"?

LUCY

I did that.

GRACE

Did you melt the butter in the microwave to soften it?

Silence.

GRACE

You did, didn't you.

LUCY

Shit.

GRACE

Start over.

LUCY

Bye.

GRACE looks out the window to the training ring.

EXT. TRAINING RING—DAY

HANK *is in the ring, riding Ransom and looking real good.*

EXT. TRAINING BARN—DAY

WYLY *and* JAMIE, *very impressed, watch from the barn.*

JAMIE

That horse is one scopey son of a gun. That's for sure.

WYLY

Well, don't you worry about him.

INT. TRAINING BARN—GRACE'S OFFICE—DAY

GRACE *sees* WYLY *and* JAMIE *watching. She watches* HANK *for a moment longer. She begins doing paperwork.* GEORGIA *sticks her head in the door. She's carrying a stack of ledgers and checkbooks.*

GEORGIA

Honey? Hi. I thought we should get caught up on the books here before it gets any crazier . . .

GRACE

Mother. Now's not a good time.

GEORGIA comes in anyway.

GEORGIA

Well then, just give me the accounts and I'll enter everything.

GRACE

Mom.

GEORGIA's not fooling anybody. They sit for a second.

GEORGIA

Honey. He slipped.

GRACE

Mother, please, I don't want to talk about this with you!

GEORGIA

Honey, it happens in the best of marriages. It doesn't mean he doesn't love you. The decisions you make now, you'll have to live with for the rest of your life. And so will Caroline.

GRACE

Are you through?

GEORGIA
(*quietly*)

You have a child that loves her daddy. And he loves her. Now, crazy as it seems, it's up to you to help him up.

GRACE

I don't believe I'm hearing this.

GEORGIA stands to leave.

GEORGIA

And I'll tell you something else. You've gone about
this in a way that everyone's gonna be talking about
for a long time. Well, you let them talk, but from now
on this is *private family business.* You need to talk, you
come talk to your mama . . .

GEORGIA waits for a response from GRACE, who stares out the window.

GEORGIA

Well, we can do these books another time . . .

GEORGIA heads to the door.

GEORGIA

I love you, honey.

EXT. EMMA RAE'S HOUSE—EVENING

*A shot of* EMMA RAE *'s house with the lights on.*

INT. EMMA RAE'S HOUSE—EVENING

EMMA RAE *walks through her living room, glancing out the window. She stops.*
EMMA RAE *'s* POINT OF VIEW *is of* EDDIE *'s car being parked behind the house. She
turns around as* GRACE *comes out of the bedroom.*

EMMA RAE

Grace. Eddie's coming.

GRACE looks like a deer caught in headlights.

GRACE

WHAT?!

EMMA RAE

Daddy must've called him. What do you want me to do?

GRACE

Well, keep him busy for a second!

She grabs her purse and storms into the bedroom, slamming the door. EMMA RAE watches EDDIE as he comes to her door. He knocks. EMMA RAE casually walks over and opens her front door. EDDIE's face holds the perfect blend of humility and concern.

EDDIE
(*quietly*)

Is she here?

EDDIE slips in and stands next to the door. EMMA RAE nods.

EMMA RAE
(*conspiratorially*)

Yeah.

She knees him in the balls as hard as she can and drops him to the floor.

EMMA RAE

I'll get her.

She strolls across the room, taps on the bedroom door and leans against the wall with her arms folded, coolly watching EDDIE struggle on the floor.

EMMA RAE
(*through the door*)

Grace? The lying cheating sack of shit is here.

A second later, GRACE opens the door. She doesn't see him immediately.

GRACE

Where?

EDDIE emits a grunt and she spots him curled up on the floor, holding his hands tightly between his legs, trying to catch his breath.

GRACE

OH MY GOD!

She runs and stands over him, not knowing what to do.

GRACE

Emma Rae? What did you do?!

EMMA RAE
(*placidly*)

You said keep him busy. He's busy holding his nuts.

EDDIE
(*squeezing the words out*)

Goddamn it!

He is struggling to his knees. His eyes wildly scan the room, making sure EMMA RAE is not nearby.

GRACE

Eddie, are you all right?!

EDDIE
(*struggling for breath*)

No goddamnit!

GRACE

Help me get him up!

EDDIE

No!! You just stay the fuck over there!

EMMA RAE

Don't worry. I wouldn't walk that far to help you up.

GRACE

Oh my God! Emma Rae, what is wrong with you?!

EMMA RAE

Consider it a blow for your dignity.

GRACE

What's dignified about kicking somebody in the balls?!

EMMA RAE

Well . . . I feel better.

She quickly walks out the door, leaving GRACE and EDDIE suddenly alone. EDDIE has made it to his feet. GRACE is really upset. A flash of panic shows in both of their eyes. GRACE turns and walks away from him.

EDDIE

Grace . . .

GRACE
(*through gritted teeth*)

What.

This is EDDIE's worst thing, talking, and he's having a lot of difficulty.

EDDIE

Look . . . I know . . .

GRACE
(*jumping on it*)

No, you don't know! You *don't* know what it's like to be *lied* to and you *don't* know what it's like to be sitting there with your child while you watch your husband makin' out with somebody on the street, and you don't know what it feels like to be made a big fat fool of in front of everybody!! . . . so please do not begin with "I know" because you DO NOT KNOW!

EDDIE exhales.

EDDIE

What I was going to say, is that I know I'm one hundred percent in the wrong here, and I don't blame you for being mad . . .

GRACE
(*bitterly*)

What a comfort.

EDDIE

Grace . . .

GRACE

I don't want this! I don't want to be this person, this *wife*! I feel like an *idiot*! Can you understand that?

EDDIE doesn't say anything.

GRACE

What if Caroline had seen you? Do you know how close she came?

EDDIE

I know. I'm sorry!

GRACE

I don't care if you're sorry! I'm not that kind of woman, Eddie, that can just let it go. That was not our deal. I want you to leave now.

EDDIE

Don't I get to say anything?

GRACE

I'd really rather you didn't.

EDDIE is frustrated at being this much in the wrong.

EDDIE

Where's the doodlebug?

GRACE

She's not here. She's with Mother.

EDDIE

You can't stop me from seeing her, Grace!

GRACE

I'm not! I didn't know you were coming! Don't make something out of nothing. She's at Aunt Rae's. If you want to see her, go over there . . . I dare you.

He stops at the door.

EDDIE

Well, will you tell her I love her?

GRACE

Whatever that means.

EDDIE

Jesus.

GRACE

I mean, Christ, Eddie. You don't even like horses.

The door slams behind him.

EXT. DRIVEWAY—EVENING

EMMA RAE *is walking back to her house.* EDDIE *is heading to his car and they are going to meet in the yard.*

>                    EDDIE

Em.

She walks past him.

>                    EDDIE

Emma Rae!

She keeps walking but turns to look at him.

>                    EMMA RAE

Are you addressing me?

>                    EDDIE

Yes!

>                    EMMA RAE

Well lick it, put a stamp on it and mail it to someone who gives a shit.

She turns away as EDDIE, in frustration, stomps off.

EXT. KING FARMS—EARLY MORNING

MONTAGE *of early morning horse activity.*

EXT. PADDOCK AREA—MORNING

CLOSE-UP *of stirrup leather being adjusted and a small boot slipping into a stirrup. Reveal* CAROLINE *on a chestnut horse named Miss Lily, a large hunter pony.* HANK *is there.* GRACE *comes in.*

> HANK

O.K., just trot around and warm up.

> GRACE
> (*brightly*)

Hey, sweetie plum!

> CAROLINE
> (*dully*)

Hey.

CAROLINE trots the horse around the paddock.

> GRACE

Is she drivin' you crazy over Possum?

> HANK
> (*brusquely*)

Nope. (*To* CAROLINE:) Keep her in a trot.

CAROLINE trots around. Possum is getting a bath in the cross ties. As she passes, she speaks to him:

> CAROLINE

Hey, Possum.

She rides around to the other side, where GRACE is. As she passes:

GRACE

Lookin' good, sweetie!

CAROLINE

Bo-ring!

HANK
(*to* CAROLINE)

Slow her just a tad.

GRACE figures out that she's not too popular around here.

GRACE

Hank, look, I've been waiting for the right opportunity to bring it up with Dad, but . . . you've gotta know
if it was up to me . . .

HANK
(*cutting her off*)

But it's not, is it. Look, Grace, I'm not gonna leave before the show, so don't worry about it. Unlike some
people, I take a certain pride in keeping my word. But
when it's over, I'm gone. Now, I've got work to do.

He walks away. CAROLINE blows by again but doesn't look at her. She
gives up and goes to the training ring to watch WYLY on Harvey.

EXT. TRAINING RING—MORNING

WYLY is on his new horse, Harvey, and JAMIE, the trainer, is in the center of the ring. The horse is absolutely beautiful. JAMIE is frustrated
because WYLY doesn't listen to a goddamn thing he says. He approaches
a jump, but at the last minute circles out.

JAMIE

Good decision . . . that's what I saw. You were right on
the half stride. Come back around and let him come
forward a little more.

GRACE walks out to the middle of the course, behind JAMIE. WYLY approaches the jump again, and again circles out.

JAMIE
(*frustrated*)

It was right there. Just come back and jump the jump.
He'll see the distance if you can't. Just support him
with your leg.

WYLY brings him around again, and this time pulls him up and stops
three or four strides before the fence.

WYLY

Son, why don't you just pipe down and let me get the
feel of him?!

JAMIE

He knows what he's doing (*under his breath:*) more than
you do, you belligerent son of a bitch.

WYLY

Son, I been doin' this since you were in short pants . . .

JAMIE
(*under his breath*)

Thank God I'm not your son, you hardheaded bastard.
You don't know your ass from Bakersfield.

WYLY has noticed GRACE and stops.

                    WYLY

Hey there!

JAMIE didn't notice GRACE at first and is embarrassed to have been overheard.

                    JAMIE

Oops.

                    GRACE

I feel for ya, buddy.

INT. KING HOUSE DINING ROOM—NOON

CLOSE-UP of a dining table. The thump of bowls of biscuits, fried
chicken, green beans, stewed tomatoes and corn pudding, basically
enough for an army, being set on the table by EULA, GEORGIA, GRACE
and EMMA RAE. WYLY comes in and takes his place at the head of the
table.

                    WYLY

Hello Mother.

Everyone is seated. WYLY bows his head for a second.

                    WYLY

Amen.

Food is passed furiously around the table.

WYLY

Where's Caroline?

GRACE

At school.

WYLY

I guess she must be missing her daddy pretty good by now.

GRACE

Yes, I'm sure she is.

WYLY

You're aware that we're involved in a real estate deal with Eddie and his dad. Emma Rae mention anything about that to you at all?

GRACE

Yes Daddy, I'm aware of it. The Wheeler Farm project. I'm very aware of it.

WYLY

So then, you know how uncomfortable it makes all of us for you and Eddie to be having these kind of problems in the middle of what could be a very lucrative situation for everyone.

GRACE
(*teeth clenched*)

Yes.

GRACE and EMMA RAE make eye contact across the table. EMMA RAE is on the case.

> WYLY
>
> I talked to Eddie again last night. He wants to make amends. He's willing to do whatever it takes to work this thing out.

> GRACE
>
> The marriage or the deal?

> WYLY
> (*warning*)
>
> Don't you get smart with me.

> EMMA RAE
>
> It's a legitimate question.

GEORGIA continues to eat, knowing the potential powder-keg situation they've got going here.

> WYLY
> (*warning*)
>
> I'm talking to your sister.

> EMMA RAE
>
> I know. I'm just following along in the conversation for the hell of it.

> WYLY
> (*to* GRACE)
>
> Under the circumstances, don't you think it would be in everybody's best interest, but especially Caroline's, for you and Eddie to sit down and talk?

GRACE

I guess that depends on who you mean by everybody.

WYLY

Now listen, honey, everybody makes mistakes. I'm not sayin' that he hasn't done anything wrong. He knows he has. But he's a good father and a good provider and that's not so easy to come by. And he has a lot of other fine qualities . . .

GRACE
(*interrupting*)

Then you marry him.

WYLY

Now listen, child! People have survived a lot worse tragedies than this. You are a grown woman with a child and responsibilities and sooner or later you're gonna have to face up to 'em! You are too old to come runnin' home! You can't work things out, that's one thing, but you haven't even tried! And that I won't have! Do you understand what I'm saying?

GRACE
(*reasonably, at first*)

I think so, Daddy. What you're telling me is that if I'd just eat shit, politely with a knife and fork . . .

GEORGIA

Oh Grace, please! . . .

GRACE
(*shouting*)

And just learn to swallow handfuls of whatever kind
of bullshit he wants to serve up to me, then everything
will just be A-O.K.!! That's it, right? That's basically
what you're saying, isn't it, Daddy?!! Isn't it?!!?

GRACE manages to hit her plate, spilling it all over her. She jumps up
from the table and storms out. The three of them are left quietly sitting there.

EMMA RAE

Nice goin', Daddy. You handled that like a pro.

WYLY

You! . . . better watch out! I have just about had it with
you!!

She stands and throws her napkin in her plate and walks out, leaving
the two of them. GEORGIA tries to fathom what goes through his mind.

WYLY
(*quietly to his wife*)

All our friends complain about how their kids grow
up and go off and they never hear from them anymore. Why in the *hell* can't that happen to us?

INT. EMMA RAE'S HOUSE—DAY

As EMMA RAE *comes charging in,* GRACE *is on her knees, rooting through her
suitcase, looking for something to wear.*

EMMA RAE

Are you all right?

GRACE
(*utterly frustrated*)

Yes! I'm just . . . What did I do? I was gonna be a goddamn large animal vet. I only had a year to go . . . And look at me. How did this happen to me?

EMMA RAE
(*incredulously*)

How did this *happen* to you?!

EMMA RAE goes over, grabs a photo album off the shelf and flips through it furiously. She drops the open photo album onto GRACE's lap. There's a picture of GRACE and EDDIE, both completely wrecked, laughing as hard as they can.

EMMA RAE

What's that?

GRACE

It's the Chi O Sadie Hawkins Dance . . .

EMMA RAE

That's *right*! Exhibit A! Sadie Hawkins! *You* asked *him*!

GRACE

SO?! What's your point!

EMMA RAE
(*frustrated*)

My *point* is . . . none of this just *happened* to you! Let's face it, Grace, you were not just hit by a truck!

GRACE

I never said that!

GRACE pulls on a pair of not-so-clean jodhpurs under her skirt and throws the skirt on the pile.

GRACE

I have to go. I have a Charity League meeting . . .

EMMA RAE

Another perfect case in point!

GRACE

Emma Rae! Contrary to whatever Daddy may say, I *am* facing up to my responsibilities. I have a *cookbook to put out,* a *daughter to raise* and the *goddamn Winter Grand Prix* and I just *don't have time* for the nervous break-down that I so desperately deserve! So please, don't ask me to stop and *think*!

EMMA RAE

No, you're right Grace. You're right. Forget it.

Frustrated, EMMA RAE turns and leaves.

GRACE
(*calling after her*)

I only asked him because he was a good dancer.

GRACE looks at the photo album, looking at herself and EDDIE in what were definitely happier times, pictures on the dance floor. There is really something going on between them in all the pictures. She flips pages. There is one really killer picture of EDDIE, flashing that killer smile. For one second, a wisp of a smile crosses Grace's lips, then back to reality. She closes the album, piles the clothes back into the suitcase and closes that too.

EXT. KING FARMS—DAY

GRACE *is driving out of the driveway. She sees* CAROLINE *jumping Miss Lily in the training ring.* HANK *is in the middle of the ring and* JAMIE *leans on the rail.* GRACE *slows down to see better.* JAMIE *turns around and sees her. They make eye contact. She holds up her hand as a wave and silently mouths the word "hi" and he does the same. She drives on out of the driveway with him watching. He then turns back to the rail and continues watching* CAROLINE *and* HANK.

INT. HALLWAY—CHARITY LEAGUE HOUSE—DAY

GRACE *is looking pretty despondent, lugging her cookbook materials but still in her barn clothes.* LORENE TUTTLE, *a very attractive brunette, comes out of a room and urgently calls to* GRACE.

> LORENE

Grace! Wait!

GRACE stops.

> LORENE
> (*whispering*)

I've been trying to call you.

She pulls GRACE aside. She seems very upset.

> GRACE

What's wrong?

LORENE
(*whispering*)

I heard . . . that you've left Eddie.

GRACE *isn't thrilled that this is common knowledge, but it must be if* LORENE
*knows.*

GRACE
(*noncommittally*)

Well, Lorene . . . You know . . .

LORENE
(*sincerely*)

Grace, you would tell me if it had anything to do with
me, wouldn't you?

GRACE

Of course I . . . (*It sinks in, but* GRACE *recovers.*) . . . would
. . . Lorene, but after all, that was . . . God . . . how long
ago was that?

LORENE

Oh God, it was just before I was pregnant with Annie,
so let's see . . .

GRACE's eyes get wide with shock.

LORENE

Oh no! Not *just* before! No. God no. Poor child, she
got Tuffy's looks and my brain. No. But before that.
You know how Tuffy was always so competitive with
Eddie. We were having a time, I mean Tuffy just
wouldn't stay put and you know how nothing makes

a man pay attention like a little competition. But I mean, that's all it was. It was nothing.

GRACE is completely and totally dumbfounded. She has absolutely no idea how to respond to this admission.

GRACE

That guy . . . has such . . . heart . . . I'm so happy he could be of use to you . . . He's so *generous* that way . . .

LORENE

I know you and Eddie will work it out. Underneath, he's a really good guy.

DISSOLVE TO:

INT. MEETING—CHARITY LEAGUE HOUSE—DAY

*A* CLOSE-UP *of* GRACE*'s face. The normal business is going on but she is lost in her own little world. The voices are blurred as* GRACE *looks around at the women in the room. The voice of* NORMA LEGGETT *comes into focus as she says:*

NORMA

. . . O.K., at this time I open the floor to any new business. Any new business?

A few hands go up. NORMA calls on someone.

MARY JANE<br>(*cheerfully*)

Anybody who wants to volunteer for the Christmas Bazaar should sign up with me or call me by the end of next week. That's all.

NORMA

Anybody else? Lucy?

GRACE's hand is rising.

LUCY

If everybody would please make a commitment to sell
at least ten raffle tickets that would be great. If you don't
think you can, we need to know, so call me or Edna.

NORMA

Grace?

GRACE stands and looks a little dazed.

GRACE

Yes . . . I was just wondering, is there anybody else here
who has fucked my husband?

A gasp from the Charity Leaguers and the room goes silent. Someone drops a pin and everybody hears it.

GRACE

Lorene was just telling me how he'd been kind enough
to help her out by sleeping with her to make Tuffy
straighten up, and I was just wondering if, you know,
this is a regular service he provides to all my friends
or what.

NORMA
(*carefully*)

Grace . . . this isn't the appropriate time . . .

GRACE
(*snapping*)

I know that, Norma! It's probably not the *appropriate time* to tell you that your husband keeps half the hookers in town in high heels either! But I'm asking anyway, if there is anyone else, who for any reason, has had any kind of sex with my goddamn husband!! I think I have a right to know!!

LUCY

Grace . . . you're losing it.

Nobody moves. Nobody breathes.

GRACE

O.K. I'll tell you what. I'll start. Mary Jane. Remember that red-headed waitress at the country club? About twenty-two, built . . . she and Calhoun, well let's just say they were more than friends. Anyway, Kitty, did you know that Bill had an affair with Dr. Davenport's dental hygienist?

The din of voices builds, and fights are breaking out all over. GRACE has to shout over the pandemonium.

GRACE

And, Eleanor, you slept with George McMurry in Antigua. Lucy told me.

LUCY leaps to her feet. Women are practically crawling over each other trying to leave.

LUCY

O.K., Grace! That's enough!

GRACE

Lucy, why shouldn't we be honest?! You're supposed
to be MY FRIENDS! And if your friends won't tell you
the truth, WHO WILL? I mean, WHO ARE WE TRY-
ING TO KID?

EXT. CHARITY LEAGUE HOUSE—DAY

*The front door of the house bursts open and women come streaming out, some
charging to their cars, some swinging their purses at others' heads, others sob-
bing uncontrollably, being supported on both sides by other women.* GRACE *walks
out slowly, with her head up, but now unencumbered by any of the cookbook
materials that she came in with.*

INT. GRACE'S KITCHEN—NIGHT

CLOSE-UP *of* EDDIE *on the phone.*

EDDIE
(*apoplectic*)

WHAT ARE YOU DOING?!

The kitchen is littered with unwashed glasses and coffee cups and the
remnants of many take-out dinners. EDDIE checks them for leftovers
as he talks.

INT. TRAINING BARN—GRACE'S OFFICE—NIGHT

GRACE *sits behind the desk with her feet up. She has* EDDIE *on speakerphone.*

EDDIE
(*offscreen, on phone*)

I mean, Jesus Christ, Grace! You probably just busted
up about everybody's marriage we know!

GRACE

Well, I'm sure you can help 'em out. You're such a goddamn Good Samaritan.

EDDIE
(*offscreen*)

Come on, Grace. We can't do this! Let's . . . get some help . . . or something! George and Trudy, they went through something like this and they worked it out!

GRACE

Trudy's on Prozac, Eddie.

EDDIE
(*offscreen; frustrated*)

Well . . . don't we know any normal people we can talk to?!

GRACE

No one springs to mind.

EDDIE
(*offscreen*)

All right, Grace! What?! Do you want a divorce?! What do you want?! I'll do whatever you say!

GRACE suddenly sits up and puts her face very close to the phone. She didn't expect this.

GRACE

A divorce?

EDDIE
(*offscreen*)

Is that what you want?

GRACE

Is that what you want?

INT. TRAINING BARN—NIGHT

CAROLINE *is standing on a step outside a horse's stall, the first stall next to the office. Because it's a barn, there are no ceilings and, unbeknownst to* GRACE, CAROLINE *can hear everything.*

EDDIE
(*offscreen, on phone;* muy frustrado)

I said I think we ought to talk! If you don't want to do that . . . then I don't know what else to do!

GRACE
(*offscreen, on phone*)

I don't know . . . Are you asking me to decide right this minute? Aren't you jumping the gun a little here?

CAROLINE stands quietly, stroking the horse and listening. JAMIE walks up and silently indicates for CAROLINE to come with him. He puts his hand on her shoulder and leads her down toward the other end of the barn, toward Possum's stall. Halfway there, head down, she stops. In stride, JAMIE picks her up and carries her the rest of the way.

INT. EMMA RAE'S HOUSE—NIGHT

CLOSE-UP *on Barbara Stanwyck* (*in a clip from* California, *the "high and mighty" scene*). *The light from the television illuminates the room. Hoover grazes for popcorn, which is strewn all across the floor.* GRACE *and* EMMA RAE *are piled on the couch watching an old Barbara Stanwyck movie.* EMMA RAE *sprays another handful of popcorn across the room. She looks over at her sister, who is lost in thought. There is a knock at the door and they both sit up and look at each other. Hoover starts barking.*

EMMA RAE

Hoover! No! Quiet!

Emma looks out the window and goes to the door, looking quizzically at GRACE.

EMMA RAE

It's Jamie.

She opens the door.

EMMA RAE

Hey, Jamie.

JAMIE

Grace here? (*Sees her.*) Oh. Hey, can I talk to you for a second?

INT. TRAINING BARN—NIGHT

*He indicates with his head to follow and they walk down to Possum's stall.* GRACE *looks in and* CAROLINE *is pretending to be asleep inside a horse blanket. She's wearing her nightgown and riding boots.* GRACE *kneels down and gently shakes her.*

GRACE
(*whispering*)

Caroline. Come on. We've gotta go.

CAROLINE

No. I'm asleep.

GRACE

Come on, honey. You can't sleep here.

CAROLINE

Yes. No! I don't want to sleep there.

GRACE

Why not?

CAROLINE

It's hot.

GRACE

We'll take the covers off. Come on.

CAROLINE

No. It stinks.

GRACE

It does not stink! Now come on.

GRACE picks up CAROLINE, who offers no assistance, so GRACE has to heave her into a position so that she can carry her. She carries her out of the stall.

INT. TRAINING BARN BREEZEWAY—NIGHT

CAROLINE*'s head is on* GRACE*'s shoulder as she carries her.*

> CAROLINE
>
> Mom? Are you gonna get a divorce?

GRACE *just keeps walking as she carries* CAROLINE *out of the barn into the dark night.*

INT. BEDROOM—NIGHT

GRACE *lies on the bed, quietly holding her daughter. She carefully unwinds her arms from around a sleeping* CAROLINE *and gets up from the bed. She goes over and closes the window. She pulls the covers up to* CAROLINE*'s chin and then tiptoes into the living room. No one's there.*

EXT. EMMA RAE*'S* HOUSE—NIGHT

JAMIE *and* EMMA RAE *are on the porch.* GRACE *comes out.*

> JAMIE
>
> Is she O.K.?

> GRACE
>
> Yes. God, thank you so much. I didn't even know she was out.

> EMMA RAE
>
> O.K. I'm going to bed. I'll see you tomorrow.

She goes inside, leaving them alone.

> JAMIE

She comes down every night. Visits Possum.

> GRACE

God, she's worse than I was.

> JAMIE

She's a great kid. Smarter 'n a tree full of owls. I . . .
wouldn't talk on that speakerphone anymore though.

GRACE realizes that CAROLINE overheard.

> GRACE

Jesus Christ. I'm unfit.

> JAMIE

No you're not. Going through this shit makes you crazy.

> GRACE

How long were you together?

> JAMIE

Ten years.

> GRACE

Did you find . . . that you lost your ability to think
rationally?

JAMIE

I'm here because of a custody battle over a horse. Does that tell you anything? I don't know. Next time I think I'd just rather get shot.

GRACE

Well. Don't sugarcoat it on my account.

JAMIE
(*laughing at himself*)

Do I sound bitter? You'd tell me . . .

GRACE

Oh no, not at all!

INT. EMMA RAE'S BEDROOM—NIGHT

GRACE *enters* EMMA RAE*'s darkened, moonlit bedroom.* EMMA RAE *is in bed.*

GRACE
(*whispering*)

Are you still up?

EMMA RAE

Not technically.

GRACE

God, that guy is so nice.

EMMA RAE

Yeah he is.

GRACE

I want to have him over for dinner sometime. You think that'd be too weird?

EMMA RAE

Why would it be weird?

GRACE

I don't know. You know.

EMMA RAE

You have people over for dinner all the time. You're the world's greatest hostess for cryin' out loud. What are you gettin' all shy about?

GRACE

I'm NOT.

She is too.

EMMA RAE

Oh I see. Well, I think you should just give him a call and ask him what he likes to eat . . . And if he says "pussy," tell him to come on over.

GRACE

Oh my God! Emma Rae! You are vile!

EMMA RAE

Well, just do something, will ya? Do something drastic.

GRACE

Oh, like I haven't already? I'm going to bed. Emma
Rae . . . I know you're disappointed in me . . .

EMMA RAE

No, no . . . for you, sweetie, not in you.

GRACE starts to leave.

EMMA RAE

Hey, sleep tight.

GRACE blows her a kiss.

INT. AUNT RAE'S HOUSE—MORNING

GRACE *looks out the kitchen window at* AUNT RAE*'s backyard.*

AUNT RAE

Well, will you take some advice from a little ol' lady?
You've got to take this bull by the horns, so to speak.
Are you gonna see him?

GRACE

We're supposed to get together to talk tonight.

AUNT RAE

Where?

GRACE

Houston's.

AUNT RAE

No. Now, see? He wants to go somewhere where he thinks you won't make a scene, although deep in his heart he knows there is no such place. No, you meet him at home. And if I were you . . .

GRACE

What?

AUNT RAE

I'd . . .

GRACE

What?

AUNT RAE

I'd make him something *special* for supper.

GRACE is stunned by the simplicity of this suggestion.

GRACE

Aunt Rae, I think it's a little more complicated than that.

AUNT RAE

I'm gonna say it again—make him something special,
that he won't forget, ever.

AUNT RAE goes over to a cabinet and takes an old recipe box out and
starts flipping through it. She quickly finds what she was looking for
and hands GRACE the card.

AUNT RAE

Here. Make him that.

GRACE
(*reading*)

Broiled salmon with mint mustard sauce. (*She mutters
further.*) A half pound salmon fillet, whole grain mustard, quarter cup olive oil, fresh mint leaves . . . one
eighth teaspoon . . . Oh my God! But this is . . .

GRACE looks in wide-eyed amazement at AUNT RAE, who says all of the
following as good-naturedly as if she was telling you a recipe for
chicken soup.

AUNT RAE

It's not lethal, not in that small dose. It will, however,
make him sick as the dog that he is. Of course, you
have to tell him that you've done it or it doesn't do
any good. I always told Lloyd if he was gonna hit me
where I lived then he could expect the same from me.
I just think of it as homeopathic aversion therapy.

GRACE

Oh my God!

AUNT RAE

Sometimes a little near-death experience helps them put things in perspective. Yes ma'am.

INT. KING HOUSE DEN—EVENING

GEORGIA *and* CAROLINE *sit in the darkened living room watching old home movies of the Grand Prix.*

CAROLINE

Who's that Gramps is on there?

GEORGIA

That's Pride's Soldier Boy.

CLOSE-UP of screen: a much younger WYLY in the show ring.

GEORGIA

This is the year he won the Upperville Grand Prix.

The light from the screen illuminates CAROLINE's face and she is completely transfixed by the imagery.
    CLOSE-UP of screen: WYLY rides his horse into the ring and up to the presenter. A shot of a much younger GEORGIA as WYLY rides by. She stands as he passes and gives him a little salute. He touches his finger to the brim of his hat in return. He poses for a photograph.

CAROLINE

Why do you always do that when Gramps rides?

GEORGIA

Do what?

CAROLINE

Stand up and give that little wave.

GEORGIA

Oh that's just a thing we do. The first time, it just happened. He just looked like Prince Charming . . . and I just stood up. After that, I don't know. I just always did it.

INT. GRACE'S KITCHEN—EARLY EVENING

*A* CLOSE SHOT *of a big piece of salmon being unwrapped.* GRACE *pulls a long shiny knife from the butcher block at the exact moment that* EDDIE *comes into the kitchen. Startled, she screams when she sees him and he screams when he sees her holding the knife. They both take a second to recover.*

GRACE

Hi.

EDDIE

Hi.

EDDIE takes his jacket off and loosens his tie.

EDDIE

What are you making?

GRACE

Salmon with mint mustard sauce.

EDDIE

Sounds good.

GRACE

Aunt Rae gave me the recipe. She assures me it's unforgettable.

EDDIE

Everything you make is unforgettable.

GRACE

Eddie, please don't start trying to charm me right off
the bat like that. That's not what this is about.

EDDIE

Excuse me. Sorry. I was trying . . . Do you want a drink?
I'm gonna get a drink.

He walks out. GRACE heaves a sigh. This is hard. EDDIE comes back in
with two bourbons and stops at the freezer to put ice in the glasses.
He hands her a drink.

GRACE

I don't know what we're doing.

EDDIE

. . . Here? Sure you do. This is the beginning of my punishment.

GRACE

Look! I didn't come here to fight! YOU SAID you wanted to get together to talk! So talk!

She turns on the Cuisinart, which whirs loudly. EDDIE turns it off.

GRACE

Oh God . . . I wasn't even gonna do this! I wasn't even gonna *get married* for god's sake!

EDDIE

Oh here we go. How many times am I gonna have to hear this?! "I was gonna be a goddamn large animal vet."

GRACE

That's right!

EDDIE

Well why the hell didn't you?!

GRACE

Because Eddie! I got pregnant! Remember?!

                    EDDIE

And what? They closed down all the veterinary schools
while you were in labor?! Nobody made you quit! And
if you didn't want to get married then why in the hell
did you do it?

                    GRACE

Why'd you ask me?!

                    EDDIE

Why'd I ask you?

                    GRACE

Yeah! You're the one who hasn't even stopped dating!

                    EDDIE

You really want to know?!

                    GRACE

Yes!

                    EDDIE

Honestly, Grace . . . I didn't think you'd say yes!

GRACE is stunned into stillness. She stands with her back to EDDIE. He
realizes he's gone too far. She stares out the window.

                    EDDIE

Grace . . . that's not exactly what I meant. That didn't
come out right . . .

GRACE

No, no. I . . . want to know.

She picks up a tiny brown bottle, measures half a teaspoon, dumps it into the green sauce in the Cuisinart and pulses it twice.

INT. GRACE'S KITCHEN—AT THE TABLE—EVENING

*The candles are dripping wax onto the table.* GRACE *sits despondently at the table, not eating.* EDDIE *eats.*

EDDIE

You think this is what I wanted? I planned it this way?

GRACE

Plan? What plan?! The way you tell it you just gambled and lost!

EDDIE

No, that's the way YOU tell it! I mean . . . I miss . . . Caroline and . . .

GRACE

You should have thought of that! Did you think about her?! What exactly goes through your mind as you're slippin' it in?!

He throws his fork down.

EDDIE

Stop it! Jesus! . . . You know, you won't believe this,

but nothing I've done has come out of any intention of hurting you!

GRACE

Oh Jesus, Eddie, give me a break!

EDDIE

Well at least . . . They don't tense up when I touch them, Grace! They don't stiffen . . .

GRACE

What are you talking about?!

EDDIE

You KNOW what I'm talking about! You never *touch me*!

GRACE

That's not . . .

EDDIE

It's true! When was the last time you laid a hand on me?!

GRACE

That's not the point!

EDDIE

It is too the goddamn point!

GRACE

Well, maybe Eddie, if you kissed me like you kissed that girl, I'd be more inclined to . . .

EDDIE

To WHAT?! to WHAT, GRACE?! You can't even say it anymore!!

GRACE

Jesus Christ, don't you try to put that on me!! There's nothing wrong with me! I have orgasms every day! I've just gotten used to having them when you're not in the room!!

She grabs her plate and jumps up from the table. She slams her plate into the sink. She grabs the counter trying to control herself. EDDIE follows right behind her.

EDDIE

Well that's great, Grace! That's exactly the point!

They both stop and catch their breath for a second.

EDDIE

Grace . . . what happened here? Listen . . . how did we get this far gone? What happened to us? That's what I want to know. That's what I've been wanting to know for a long time! . . . I know I'm a disappointment! I'm a disappointment to myself! You think this is who I want to be? . . . All my life I've done exactly what was expected of me! I work for my father, for god's sake!

And so do you! I mean, Grace . . . we've both turned into exactly who we swore we'd never become! What happened?! We used to *like* each other! We used to laugh! What happened to that? What happened to Sunday under the covers? To dancing in the den after Caroline was asleep . . . and making love after two hours of sleep? I mean, Grace . . . what happened to *you* wanting *me*? I'm not one of those guys . . . This is me . . . you know me! I'm a decent guy . . .

GRACE watches, unable to move, her heart breaking for them both. Then suddenly she realizes what she's done . . .

GRACE
(*tentatively*)

Eddie . . . Eddie, I've done something . . . so wrong. I was trying . . .

EDDIE

Forget it, Grace. It doesn't matter . . .

GRACE

No, no it does . . .

She goes to him.

EDDIE

Oh God, I don't feel good . . .

GRACE

Eddie, I think we need to go to the hospital . . .

He looks up at her with the helpless expression of a dog.

GRACE

. . . there's something in the fish.

EDDIE<br>(not understanding)

What? What're you saying?

EDDIE'S POINT OF VIEW is of GRACE trying to get him up out of the chair.

GRACE

I was trying to . . .

GRACE is suddenly covered in vomit.

EDDIE

Oh my God!

GRACE<br>(panicking)

Come on! We need . . . I think we should get your
stomach pumped!

EDDIE

It's pumping itself Grace!

GRACE

Oh my God! Come on!

EDDIE is really, really sick!

> GRACE

Oh my God. What've I done?

DISSOLVE TO:

INT. HOSPITAL WAITING ROOM—NIGHT

GRACE *is sitting despondently, alone in a tiny waiting area. She is a mess, still covered with now-dry vomit. She sees* GEORGIA *make an inquiry at the nurses' station and starts trying to clean herself up.* GEORGIA *comes in and looks at* GRACE. *She is grim.*

> GEORGIA

Oh my God. Look at you. Is he all right?

GRACE nods. She looks pathetic.

> GEORGIA

What in the name of God has gotten into you? How could you listen to that silly old woman?

GRACE doesn't reply. GEORGIA takes out a handkerchief and starts trying to clean GRACE's face. GRACE pulls away. GEORGIA pulls GRACE into a bathroom

INT. HOSPITAL BATHROOM—NIGHT

> GRACE

Mother . . .

> GEORGIA

Don't you Mother me. You are an absolute mess, child.

GRACE grabs the handkerchief away from her mother.

> GRACE
> (*angrily*)

That's right, Mother! I'm a mess! Look at me!

GEORGIA is shocked by GRACE's demeanor. GRACE is really falling apart.

> GRACE
> (*full of self-loathing*)

I'm an outrage. I'm a disgrace. I'm a failure.

> GEORGIA

Grace! Don't talk like that! No you're not!

> GRACE

Yes! I AM! I drive away and forget my child. I've failed at all of it! Eddie, myself, everything! I've accomplished nothing! Nothing!

> GEORGIA

Honey, stop!

> GRACE

No! I've fucked up everything I've ever touched!

> GEORGIA
> (*intensely*)

Now you just get a grip on yourself!

GRACE turns and leaves. GEORGIA follows.

GEORGIA

This is not just about you! Do you hear what I'm saying? You have your daughter to think of! Is this what
you want her to see? Is it?

She shakes GRACE once. Hard.

GEORGIA

I'll tell you . . . I've had my own troubles. It was a long
time ago and I never wanted to saddle you with my
problems, but if ever you were to find out, I wanted
to be sure you girls would be proud of the way I
handled myself.

GRACE looks at her mother in sheer disbelief.

GRACE

Proud? Are you out of your mind? How the hell were
we supposed to be *proud* that you were oblivious to
what was going on right in front of your face!

GEORGIA

What in the name of God are you talking about? Nothing ever went on "right in front of my face"!

GRACE

Oh come on! Jesus, Mother, you were right there!
What about Mrs. Pritchett? Annie Pritchett! Are you
gonna tell me that you didn't know about that?! If
nothing else, at least Caroline will know that I didn't
just lie down like a goddamn doormat and let Eddie
walk all over me! How could you think I'd be proud?

GEORGIA is rendered utterly speechless. As she and GRACE look at each other, she slowly pulls her handkerchief from GRACE's hand, puts it in her purse, and rushes from the room.

GRACE

Mom, wait!

INT. HOSPITAL HALLWAY—NIGHT

GRACE *goes after her into the hallway, but* GEORGIA *has pushed her way into a crowded elevator.* GRACE *sees her mother's eyes, stung with tears, as the doors slide closed.* GRACE *covers her face with her hands, understanding the blow she has just dealt to her mother. She takes a deep breath and ambles down the hall to the open door of* EDDIE*'s room.*

INT. EDDIE'S HOSPITAL ROOM—NIGHT

GRACE *stands in the doorway, looking at* EDDIE, *his eyes closed, looking pale and weak. His eyes flutter open as he sees* GRACE. *He lifts his arm out to her, beckoning her to his bedside. She approaches slowly and he gently pulls her to him, his lips to her ear as he whispers:*

EDDIE

Get a lawyer.

INT. WYLY'S CAR—NIGHT

WYLY *is singing along to a country song as he puts his blinker on to turn into his driveway. A van with the word* LOCKSMITH *painted on the side is waiting to pull out. The driver gives* WYLY *a friendly wave as he passes.*

EXT. KING HOUSE—NIGHT

WYLY *climbs the front steps of the darkened house and finds the front door locked. He tries his key, which doesn't work. He checks it, tries again and, frustrated, pounds on the door.*

INT. KING HOUSE—NIGHT

GEORGIA *stands quietly on the other side of the door.*

EXT. KING HOUSE—NIGHT

WYLY *rattles the door hard again.*

> WYLY
>
> Mother! Something's wrong with this goddamn door!

> GEORGIA
> (*offscreen*)
>
> There's nothing wrong with the door. And don't call
> me Mother!

He's startled by the fact that she's right on the other side of the door.

> WYLY
>
> Then open the goddamn thing.

> GEORGIA
> (*offscreen; with conviction*)
>
> You go to hell.

WYLY is taken aback by the sound of her voice.

> WYLY
>
> Georgia? What's goin' on? Open the door.

> GEORGIA
> (*offscreen*)
>
> Why don't you go try Annie Pritchett's door?

WYLY cocks his head quizzically at the door.

                    WYLY

What in the hell are you talking about? Have you been
into the apple wine?

The front door opens a couple of inches but the chain is on it.

                    GEORGIA

I'm talking about your extracurricular activities!
I'm talking about your lying and cheating extracurricular . . .

                    WYLY
                 (*interrupting*)

Now, wait a minute. I do not cheat! I may have fooled
around a little, but I have never cheated!

                    GEORGIA

How could you do it, Wyly?! Annie Pritchett was a
friend of mine! I'm on the church auxiliary with that
woman! And the girls! Grace and Emma Rae . . .

                    WYLY

Open the door, honey.

                    GEORGIA

They think I'm a *fool*! And I am! All the years . . . And
there were times, Wyly, when I had *thoughts,* but never
once, out of respect for you and our marriage! And
now, I wish I had! I have been an utter fool!

WYLY

Now don't say that! You're not a fool, honey! . . . What thoughts?

GEORGIA

Dr. Lewis! Frank Lewis! Do you know after all these years, he still has feelings for me! Especially since his wife died! He said . . . he said I have beautiful hips!

WYLY smiles to himself. He is having a hard time taking this seriously.

WYLY

Honey, I wouldn't hang any hopes on something somebody said forty years ago.

GEORGIA

*Last week* he said it! When I took Aunt Rae in, I had my yearly physical. He said it last week!

This takes the grin off WYLY's face.

WYLY

All right, that's enough! Open the goddamn door! I've been workin' like a hired hand all day!

GEORGIA

The only thing you've been workin' all day is your big mouth!

He slams himself into the front door. The chain pulls tight.

WYLY

You open up right now! I won't tolerate this kind of
disrespect after the day I've had!

He throws himself, hard, into it again.

GEORGIA

Don't you talk to *me* about disrespect! You don't even
know the meaning of the word! You self-centered old
goat!

WYLY

Self-centered?! Who the hell do you think you're talking to? Haven't I given you every goddamn thing
you've ever wanted! You think you'd have had this
kind of life with Frank Lewis?

GEORGIA slams the door shut, pulls the chain off and opens the door
wide. She blocks the entry with her body.

GEORGIA
(*with intensity*)

The life I'd have had with Frank Lewis would include
respect! My own daughters are ashamed of me! But
I'll tell you something. I'm ashamed of *you*! You are
an embarassment! Our Grace, her life is falling apart
and all you can tell her is it's bad for business! You're
a disgrace! You drink too much! You laugh too loud
at your own jokes and I'm gonna tell you something,
Wyly! You fart in your sleep! But I've accepted every
one of your faults without complaint because they're
a part of you and I loved you! I was proud to be your
wife. But now I am *not* proud! So if you have to come

into this house, then so be it. But you better know that
if you step across this threshold, I'm gonna call down
to that barn and have those boys come up and throw
you out on your ass!!

They stand off for a moment and WYLY does not make a move. GEORGIA
steps back and the door slams shut under its own weight.

INT. KING HOUSE—LATE NIGHT

GEORGIA, AUNT RAE, EMMA RAE *and* EULA *are in the dimly lit kitchen, all silent.
There's a tap at the back door.* EMMA RAE *opens it and a ragged* GRACE *comes in.*

EMMA RAE

You missed a really good time. Although I hear you
had quite a party yourself.

GRACE

The bug?

EMMA RAE

Upstairs.

GRACE and her mother look at each other, understanding what a giant
goddamn mess this whole thing is. GRACE goes to her.

GRACE

Mother, please, I'm . . .

GEORGIA puts her fingers to GRACE's lips, looking at her and shaking her
head to say "not necessary," and GRACE, in wonderment at her mother's
ability to forgive, presses GEORGIA's fingers to her lips to kiss them.

EULA

After thirty-eight years, a little break'll do us all some
good.

AUNT RAE

Is he still roamin' around out in the yard?

GRACE

Yeah.

GEORGIA

Why doesn't he just go to a motel?

EMMA RAE

It's a territorial thing, Mama. He's probably out there
pissin' on trees.

This causes all the women to quietly chortle.

EXT. KING HOUSE—NIGHT

*A* LONG SHOT *of the house; all interior and exterior lights are on. And they're
home.* FADE TO BLACK.

EXT. KING FARMS—DAY

FADE IN: *The large King Farms trailer is being loaded with canvas awnings,
brass plaques, furniture, clothes racks and, of course, horses.* GRACE *comes out
of her office and sees* CAROLINE *again plying Possum with carrots. She goes
over and lifts her down off the mounting step.* HANK *is overseeing the loading
of horses.* DUB, *and all the grooms, are working.* JAMIE *is also loading his truck*

*with his tack boxes. He watches* GRACE *pass by, lugging stuff from her office.* GRACE *is loading boxes of registration paperwork, rider numbers, etc., into* EMMA RAE*'s car. A* LONG SHOT *of the cars and trailers rolling out of the driveway.*

EXT. COUNTRY ROAD—DAY

*The King Farms caravan is rolling along toward the show grounds.*
     EMMA RAE *is driving,* GRACE *is keeping her head turned, looking out the window.* EMMA RAE *can see* GRACE *is crying in the side-view mirror. She looks at* GRACE *and then back at the road.*

> EMMA RAE
>
> Oh Grace. I wish I could help you.

> GRACE
>
> Me too.

> EMMA RAE
>
> I could get you drunk.

> GRACE
>
> O.K.

INT. UPSCALE RESTAURANT—DUSK

*A* CLOSE SHOT *of a highball glass. The hand of an older gentleman picks up the glass and sips his bourbon and soda. This is* JACK "MAD DOG" PIERCE, *the Marvin Mitchelson of the Carolinas. He takes notes with one hand and sips from his glass with the other.* EDDIE, *sitting across the table, fidgets uncomfortably.*

JACK

Irreconcilable differences. Sounds better than "no-body cares anymore and we just want it over with." Wouldn't you say?

EDDIE

I'd say that sums it up.

JACK

What would she say?

EDDIE shifts uncomfortably in his chair.

EDDIE

She'd say I was cheatin' on her.

JACK

Were you?

EDDIE stares into his beer and exhales slowly.

JACK

Are you seeing anybody now?

EDDIE

No! Absolutely, no.

JACK

Yeah, it's not as much fun when your marriage is banging on the rocks, is it? Speaking of which . . .

JACK gestures to a waitress with his empty glass.

> EDDIE
> (*to himself*)

It was never much fun . . .

A loud whoop goes up from a nearby table. EDDIE looks over at a party of overaged frat boys and underaged secretaries.

> JACK

Does she drink?

> EDDIE

No.

JACK looks up significantly.

> JACK

She doesn't drink alcohol at all?

> EDDIE

Well . . . wine . . . sometimes.

> JACK

So she drinks.

> EDDIE

Don't write that down. Grace is not a drinker!

JACK

Was she drinking when she made the attempt on your life?

EDDIE

It wasn't an attempt on my life. It was an attempt on . . . my other life.

JACK

What about your daughter? How's she gonna like only seeing her daddy every other weekend?

EDDIE

Grace wouldn't do that. She wouldn't do it to Caroline.

JACK

Just you wait and see. She'll use that kid to take everything you've got.

EDDIE

You don't know her.

JACK

Wake up, Eddie. Divorces don't happen in church, see what I'm sayin'? No guts, no glory.

EDDIE gets up from the table.

EDDIE

Yeah, I see what you're saying. Uhh, Jack, this whole
thing has been a big mistake. Sorry I wasted your time.

He turns and leaves.

INT. LOUD BAR—NIGHT

*The bar is crowded with horse people.* GRACE *sits alone at a small table.* EMMA
RAE *is standing not far away, talking to a tall guy who obviously likes her
very much. Even though* GRACE *smiles and says hello to people she knows, she
looks very uncomfortable. She turns around to get* EMMA RAE*'s attention, who,
without taking her eyes off the guy, holds up one finger to* GRACE, *as if saying
"just a minute." For the first time,* GRACE *looks hopelessly forlorn. She sits quietly
and it just starts welling up inside her. She knows she's crumbling and that
she's going to cry and she doesn't know whether to hide her face or get up and
run to the bathroom. Suddenly* JAMIE *sits down, leans over to her and says:*

JAMIE

O.K., just act like I just said something so funny you're
about to die . . .

And with that GRACE starts to shake all over, she's laughing and crying. He leans over to her and whispers.

JAMIE

I'll just sit here like I'm waiting to zing another one
in there.

And he does look like that. Tears are streaming down her face. It really
does look like she's laughing so hard, she's about to lose it. She wipes
her tears with a napkin. And now she's so giddy, she really is laughing and crying. EMMA RAE comes over to the table.

EMMA RAE

What's so funny?

GRACE is still shaking uncontrollably and shakes her head as if to say, "I can't talk."

JAMIE

I just have that effect on people.

GRACE's head flops onto the table as she continues her jag. EMMA RAE leans over to ask her something.

EMMA RAE

Hey, Grace, uh, do you think you could get a ride home, 'cause, um . . .

EMMA RAE looks back at the guy she was talking to. JAMIE picks up on what's going on.

JAMIE
(*to* EMMA RAE)

I got it.

EMMA RAE

Oh, good. Thanks. (*To* GRACE:) I'll see you tomorrow. (*To* JAMIE, *behind* GRACE's *back, she quietly mouths:*) I wouldn't let her drink any more.

EMMA RAE motions with her head for the guy to follow her. As they pass the table, GRACE, now laughing, picks up her head and says:

GRACE

Have fun!

After they've passed, she collapses back into tears. JAMIE sits for a moment to see if she pulls it together. She doesn't.

JAMIE

Oh boy. Well, I don't know about you, but I've had about all the fun I can stand. Whaddya say we head out of here. O.K.? O.K.

He stands and helps GRACE up and they make their way out of the bar.

INT. JAMIE'S TRUCK—NIGHT

GRACE, *looking fairly wrung out, rests her head against the passenger-side door. She puts her face out the window and feels the wind. Now she's studying* JAMIE *as he drives. Bonnie Raitt is singing on the radio.*

GRACE

Is this a tape?

JAMIE

Yeah.

JAMIE turns into the King Farms driveway. He stops in front of EMMA RAE's house. GRACE doesn't move to get out.

JAMIE

Is this where you wanted to go?

GRACE

No.

JAMIE

Oh. Well. Where do you want to go?

GRACE

I don't know. I don't feel like going home yet.

JAMIE

Well . . . I'd invite you back to my place for a night-cap if . . .

GRACE

O.K.

JAMIE

O.K.

INT. JAMIE'S HOUSE—NIGHT

*The door creaks open and* GRACE *and* JAMIE *step into the small tenant house, which* JAMIE *keeps as neat as a pin. There is a shirt on the floor, which* JAMIE *self-consciously picks up and rolls into a ball.*

GRACE

Wow. It's been a long time since I've been in here.

JAMIE

Wasn't expecting company.

GRACE takes the shirt out of his hand and throws it back on the floor. She walks around the small room, looking at everything.

GRACE

God. Everything seems smaller.

JAMIE

Yeah, it's kind of close quarters in here. You want a drink?

GRACE

Yeah. I used to play in here when I was little. And then later . . .

JAMIE

I think there's some glasses here somewhere.

He's opening and closing cabinets until he finds them.

GRACE

. . . I lost something in here . . .

He pours two bourbons and hands her a glass. She clinks her glass to his, knocks back her whole shot and hands him back her glass. He stands motionless, holding his full shot and her empty. She goes over to the window.

GRACE

God, I was sixteen, fifteen, no sixteen because that was the year I rode Miracle Child in the National. He was here with his parents. Everybody was off at the auction . . .

JAMIE

Umm . . . would you like another drink?

She nods and he hands her his full glass. This time she just sips it.

GRACE

I remember I was so nervous. I was standing right here in this very spot, with my back to him, looking out the window. I knew I wanted something to happen, but I didn't know what to do or say . . . so I just stood here, hoping and waiting . . . for him to make his move.

JAMIE

And?

JAMIE comes up behind her and she feels his arms come around her waist. She closes her eyes and takes a deep breath.

GRACE

And finally . . . he did.

And with that GRACE turns and flings her arms around JAMIE, kissing him passionately. She pushes him onto the bed, causing him to hit his head on the wall.

GRACE
(*between kisses*)

Sorry.

She starts unbuttoning his shirt, fervently at first, but her enthusiasm diminishes with each button until finally she is still. He is still ardent, but notices that she has stopped moving.

> JAMIE
> (*whispering*)

What's wrong?

> GRACE

Nothing. Nothing.

She pops the last button on his shirt and, frustrated, leaps up off the bed, shouting:

> GRACE

Fuck you Eddie! Fuck you!

JAMIE, startled out of his wits, is looking around for EDDIE.

> GRACE

I have absolutely *nothing* to feel guilty about! I was not the one who was unfaithful! Right? Am I right?

> JAMIE

Right.

She comes back to the bed, takes his shirt off and starts unbuttoning her own shirt.

> GRACE
> (*with conviction*)

I mean, I *want* to do this! I really want to!

JAMIE starts to kiss her again. Gently.

JAMIE

Good.

He helps her with her buttons. She starts to get back into it. He slips her shirt off, so she is now in her jeans and camisole. They lie back on the bed, but as soon as her head touches the pillow, she's up again, talking to EDDIE.

GRACE

But you know, it just figures that the one time I would want to do this, you'd figure out a way to take the fun out of it! I am *not* doing this for revenge!

She points emphatically at JAMIE.

GRACE

You are *not* a revenge fuck! Let's just get that straight right now!

JAMIE

O.K.

GRACE

That is *not* what's going on here!

JAMIE takes a deep breath.

JAMIE

What *is* going on here?

GRACE

I have absolutely no idea . . .

JAMIE

Come here.

She goes and sits on the bed. He puts his arm around her.

GRACE

I mean, this is crazy. I've been wanting this . . .

JAMIE

Well, I can't believe I'm about to say this, but . . . you
are not ready.

GRACE

Oh yes I am.

JAMIE
(*resigned*)

Oh no you're not. Listen, I know about this. You're
gonna have to face facts. You've got a broken heart
and you've gotta deal with it. And, I don't want to be
this crazy thing you did one night.

GRACE

Are you sure?

JAMIE responds as cheerfully as any man who is about to turn down an
almost certain opportunity to sleep with a beautiful woman who hasn't

been laid in a really long time. He emits an ironic yelp. GRACE sits with
her head in her hands.

> GRACE

Shit . . . Well . . . then what do you want to do?

> JAMIE

I don't know. What do you want to do?

INT. KING HOUSE KITCHEN—NIGHT

*A refrigerator light illuminates the kitchen.* JAMIE *is moaning in ecstasy.* GRACE
*is quietly laughing and shushing him.*

> JAMIE

Oh God. MMMmmm, God.

GRACE is heading to the table with two huge glasses of milk. In front
of JAMIE is an entire pecan pie, which he and GRACE are sharing. GRACE
is relaxed and happy and smiling.

> JAMIE

I'll say one thing, you Southern women sure are easy
to please.

> GRACE
> (*laughing*)

I guess that's what comes from centuries of being bred
to keep your expectations low.

GRACE stops laughing.

GRACE

Oh my God.

INT. KING HOUSE—NIGHT

GRACE *charges noiselessly up the stairs to a bedroom door.*

INT. KING HOUSE BEDROOM—NIGHT

CAROLINE *lies fast asleep in a twin bed. The moonlight falls across the covers as* GRACE *slips into the room. She gently, but urgently, wakes her up.*

GRACE

Caroline. Wake up. I have to tell you something.

CAROLINE, completely dazed, sits up.

GRACE

You're going to ride Possum. O.K.?

CAROLINE throws back the covers and stands up.

GRACE

Not right now sweetie. Tomorrow.

CAROLINE gets right back in bed.

GRACE

Do you know I love you, bug?

CAROLINE

Yes.

GRACE

All right baby. Good night.

CAROLINE

Good night.

GRACE kisses her and tiptoes out of the room, closing the door behind her. As she's quietly making her way down the stairs, a satisfied "Yes!" from CAROLINE's room.

EXT. SHOW GROUNDS—DAY

*The same caravan of trucks and trailers is now part of the large traffic jam going into the show grounds. A large sign welcomes them to the exhibitors' gate of the Winter National Grand Prix.*

EXT. KING FARMS GRAND PRIX SHOW BARN—LATE AFTERNOON

*The barn is decorated with King Farms awnings and the area around the entrance is landscaped. There is a sitting area with leather chairs and a full bar.*
    CAROLINE *is having the finishing touches put on her by a very dressed-up* GRACE *and* EMMA RAE. HANK *is dressed in his riding suit too. The three of them are nervous wrecks compared to the serene bearing of* CAROLINE.

| EMMA RAE | GRACE |
|---|---|
| Now, he has a tendency to back off at the first fence, so keep him in front of your leg . . . | . . . and trot him all the way to the end and let him see the course . . . |

CAROLINE
(*spotting* EDDIE)

Hi Daddy!

EDDIE gives her a big smile as she goes running up to him.

EDDIE

Hey doodlebug! Look at you! You look like a winner!

He gives CAROLINE a big, extra-long hug and a kiss. She kisses him five times and then runs back to EMMA RAE. GRACE is just standing there. This is the first time they've been together since the hospital, so it's . . . uncomfortable.

EDDIE

Grace.

GRACE

Hi Eddie.

HANK comes up with Possum to fetch CAROLINE.

HANK

Ready Caroline?

CAROLINE

Come on Daddy!

EDDIE

I'm right behind you, sweetie.

EDDIE follows them. EMMA RAE continues talking to CAROLINE to cover the awkwardness of the moment.

EXT. KING FARMS SHOW BARN—DAY

CAROLINE *is already mounted on Possum.*

> EMMA RAE
>
> From three to four is a bending line. It's set on the half stride and . . . You'll feel him going into it so just support him at the vertical . . .

> EDDIE
>
> O.K. ladybug. I'm gonna go watch. Go in there and . . .

EMMA RAE looks at him as if to say "What could you possibly tell her about being in that ring?"

> EDDIE
>
> . . . have fun.

He goes over and gives her a big squeeze and a kiss.

> EDDIE
>
> I'll see you out there.

As EDDIE leaves, GRACE comes up.

> GRACE
>
> Now, just focus and listen to Hank and you'll be . . .

CAROLINE
(*frustrated*)

Mom. Please . . . just . . . go watch. O.K.? I wanna do it
by myself.

GRACE and EMMA RAE both look at HANK, who fully understands they are
trusting him with CAROLINE's life. GRACE leans down and hugs her.

GRACE
(*whispering*)

You come from a long line of winners, honey. Me and
your Aunt Em, we used to run this joint.

CAROLINE

Just watch.

INT. KING FARMS BOX—SHOW RING STANDS—LATE AFTERNOON

GRACE, EMMA RAE, GEORGIA *and* AUNT RAE *sit in a box in the arena that is
right on the rail. They're nervous as the horses from the last class clear the
ring.* WYLY *arrives in the box and sits in a seat at the back.* GEORGIA *knows
he's there but doesn't acknowledge him.*

ANNOUNCER
(*offscreen*)

All right ladies and gentleman, coming into the ring is
our next class, number ninety-three, the twenty-five-
hundred-dollar Winter National Youth Jumper Classic!

GRACE and GEORGIA exchange a glance, GRACE finally knowing what her
mother has been through a hundred times.

GEORGIA

Don't forget to breathe.

GRACE scans the crowd, looking for EDDIE. She spots him and tries to make eye contact, but to EDDIE, she may as well be invisible. He smiles and says hello to people he knows.

INT. HOLDING AREA OUTSIDE RING—LATE AFTERNOON

*All the horses and riders are waiting in the warm-up ring. We see the horses in all their glory, tails flowing, manes braided. The riders are all dressed in their finest.* CAROLINE *is on Possum with* HANK *holding his bridle. She is the youngest and smallest of the entrants. In the background we can see a youth rider doing the course.*

HANK

It's about that time.

HANK looks at CAROLINE, who indicates that she's ready. He leads her toward the ring.

**CLOSE SHOTS OVER MUSIC:**

Of him giving her a pat on the leg as we ride with CAROLINE into the packed arena.

Of CAROLINE's face, pure concentration, much like GRACE's face when she rides.

Of Possum sailing easily over a jump.

Of the blowing nostrils of the horse as she puts him through his paces.

Of GRACE watching EDDIE, who's only looking at CAROLINE.

Of HANK's eyes riveted to her.

Of GRACE and EMMA RAE's eyes watching every move, and their lips moving in silent instructions.

Of EDDIE watching GRACE watch their daughter.

HANK<br>(to himself)

That's it, that's it, don't over-ride him . . .

INT. SHOW RING—LATE AFTERNOON

She lines up and takes the last series of jumps and makes every one of them clean as can be. The crowd roars its approval and CAROLINE has a wide grin as she pats Possum on his sweaty neck.

> ANNOUNCER
> (*offscreen*)

And that's a clean round for number one-oh-five . . .

INT. KING FARMS BOX—LATE AFTERNOON

> GEORGIA
> (*quietly to* GRACE)

There you go honey, there's your accomplishment.

From GRACE's expression, you can see how much she wishes she could feel that way.

> GRACE

Mom . . . that's not my accomplishment. It's hers.

INT. SHOW RING—LATE AFTERNOON

> ANNOUNCER

Announcing the awards for the 1995 Winter National twenty-five-hundred-dollar Youth Jumper Classic. Carrying on that family tradition, first place goes to number one-oh-five, Caroline Bichon riding Silver Bells!

CAROLINE rides Possum around the ring to the winner's circle. HANK comes up, while the presenters are positioned holding a big silver tray. As HANK puts the ribbon on Possum's bridle and the sash is hung around his neck, CAROLINE, smiling, says:

CAROLINE

I told you I was ready.

HANK
(*proud and smiling*)

Oh, I knew it. All along.

INT. SHOW RING STANDS—LATE AFTERNOON

WYLY, *boasting to all who will listen.*

WYLY

That's my granddaughter!

EDDIE, watching CAROLINE, so proud.

INT. SHOW RING—LATE AFTERNOON

ANNOUNCER

Let's hear it one more time for our youth riders and
our champion Caroline Bichon on Silver Bells as they
take their victory gallop!

CAROLINE rides once more, leading the other riders who have also won
ribbons, cantering around the ring as the crowd cheers. As she approaches her mother's box, she touches the brim of her hat, and all
together, the whole King family stands as she passes and gives her a
little salute.

EXT. KING FARMS SHOW BARN—LATE AFTERNOON

*The King family is headed en masse back to their barn, however, they're not
exactly a cohesive unit.* WYLY *catches up to* GEORGIA, *who is walking with* AUNT

RAE. *He tries to drape his arm around her shoulder, but she dips ever so slightly to come out from under it.* CAROLINE *is* so *excited. She walks with* HANK, *who is leading the horse.*

GRACE

Caroline! Come here for a minute!

CAROLINE runs over and hugs GRACE. GRACE pins a tiny gold horse to Caroline's riding coat.

GRACE

Mama gave me this the first time I won in my fourteen-and-under class.

CAROLINE

It's beautiful . . .

They hug . . . tight.

GRACE

I'm proud of you, baby.

CAROLINE

I'm proud of you too, Mom.

GRACE
(*smiling*)

For what?

CAROLINE
(*smiling back*)

For . . . doing the right thing.

CAROLINE kisses GRACE.

CAROLINE

DADDY!!

CAROLINE runs to EDDIE, who picks her up and spins her around, hugging and kissing her. GRACE follows as they head to the barn. WYLY, at the bar, with drink in hand, commandeers CAROLINE as if she were his protégé. He shows her off and regales the barn visitors with tales of her glory. GEORGIA graciously greets all the visitors and well-wishers and points them to the bar.

INT. KING FARMS SHOW BARN—LATE AFTERNOON

GRACE *and* EDDIE *are both watching* CAROLINE, *filled with love and pride.*

GRACE

Hey, pretty great, huh?

EDDIE

Yeah, I mean . . . incredible . . .

GRACE

Did you see how she just knew? . . .

EDDIE

I did.

They look at each other, sweet and then awkward. And GRACE notices that EDDIE is slightly choked up.

EDDIE

. . . you know it's just hard, not seeing her . . .

GRACE

She misses you too. Maybe she should go home with you tonight.

EDDIE
(*surprised*)

Really?

GRACE

She's gonna want to come see Daddy ride tomorrow . . .

EDDIE

I'll bring her back to you in the morning . . .

GRACE

You can just bring her back here for the show . . .

EDDIE

O.K. Thanks.

They look at each other sadly. They make a move to hug or kiss or some kind of typical affection, but they self-consciously catch themselves and stop.

GRACE

Well . . . um, bye . . .

She leaves.

EXT. SHOW BARN—LATE AFTERNOON

AUNT RAE *and* GEORGIA *sit by and let* EMMA RAE *pour champagne for them.* AUNT RAE *and* EMMA RAE *perform the following ritual: As* EMMA RAE *pours:*

> AUNT RAE
>
> Just a little drop, now . . . more . . . a little more . . . just a skosh more . . . keep going . . .

Her glass is now full to the top.

> AUNT RAE
>
> That's good.

GRACE drifts for a second, then snaps out of it and goes looking for HANK. He is packing stuff into a bag.

> GRACE
>
> Hank. I've got to talk to you.

He doesn't even acknowledge her presence. She pushes him into a tack room and closes the door. DISSOLVE TO:

INT. KING HOUSE BEDROOM—NIGHT

*The room is dimly lit and* AUNT RAE, *looking wan, is propped up in bed, but asleep. Dr. Frank Lewis, a lanky silver-haired gentleman, stands removing his stethoscope. He indicates quietly to a worried* GEORGIA *that everything's O.K. They move to leave the room.*

EXT. KING HOUSE—NIGHT

*A drunken* WYLY *is pacing around in the front yard and checking the bedroom window for signs of motion. He sees their shadows cross the window.*

INT. KING HOUSE DARKENED LIVING ROOM—NIGHT

GRACE *and* EMMA RAE *sit in the dark, on each end of the sofa, watching* WYLY *through the window. Unaware that he's being watched, he's talking to himself, shadowboxing and bumping into shrubbery and other fixed objects.*

EMMA RAE

He is the silliest son of a bitch on two legs, isn't he?

GRACE

That's a roger.

EXT. KING HOUSE—NIGHT

WYLY *finally sees the front door open, and* FRANK *and* GEORGIA *are talking quietly. He hears* GEORGIA *softly chuckling.* DR. LEWIS *comes out on the porch and* WYLY *trots up to the door, ostensibly to try to get in, at least on the conversation, but* GEORGIA*'s fast and the front door closes and locks.*

WYLY

Well, Doc, is she O.K.?

FRANK

Oh yeah. You get to be that age and you get a little excitement, have a little too much punch, but she's O.K. She'll outlive us all.

WYLY

Well, that's good. That's fine.

DR. LEWIS waits for him to say something else but he doesn't.

FRANK

Well, call me if you need to. And good luck tomorrow night . . .

WYLY looks preoccupied.

INT. KING HOUSE BEDROOM—NIGHT

*A perfectly healthy and alert* AUNT RAE *tries to see what's going on out the
window.*

EXT. KING HOUSE—NIGHT

WYLY

Hey, Doc? . . . Did you say she had beautiful hips?

FRANK

Well . . . Yes I did. I meant for . . . Well, she does. And
you know I delivered both your girls so I've seen . . .

WYLY hauls off and swings, haymaker style, at DR. LEWIS, who nimbly
steps out of the way and lets WYLY fall to the ground.

INT. KING HOUSE LIVING ROOM—NIGHT

GRACE, EMMA RAE *and* GEORGIA *all see it.*

GEORGIA

Oh my Lord!

GRACE

Stay here, Mama!

GRACE and EMMA RAE run outside.

EXT. KING HOUSE—NIGHT

WYLY *jumps up and* DR. LEWIS *assumes a boxing pose.*

FRANK

It's all right! I boxed in the Navy!

GRACE grabs WYLY.

GRACE

Daddy, stop it! Jesus Christ!

INT. KING HOUSE—NIGHT

AUNT RAE *hears footsteps and scampers back to bed. She's resumed her prostrate pose as* EULA *looks in.*

EXT. KING HOUSE—NIGHT

WYLY *is still blowing hard as* DR. LEWIS *drives away.* GRACE *and* EMMA RAE *are on the porch, too.* WYLY, *weaving unsteadily, trips and lands hard in a sitting position on the steps.*

WYLY
(*drunkenly*)

That sonofabitch better not come around here 'less he wants to get his ass kicked. He's a *no good* sonofabitch.

GRACE and EMMA RAE look at each other and go over and pull WYLY up to a standing position.

EMMA RAE

C'mon, Daddy. There's more ass to kick tomorrow. You can rack out at my house tonight.

With his arms around their shoulders, they start walking him around the house, the gravel crunching under their footsteps.

WYLY

Can't even sleep in my own goddamn bed.

GRACE

Daddy, I talked to Hank tonight.

WYLY

Good. You get him all squared away?

GRACE

Yeah.

WYLY

He's not gonna quit?

GRACE

No.

WYLY

Good.

GRACE

Because he's riding Ransom.

The three of them all stop.

WYLY

What? . . . Now why would you go and say a fool thing like that?!

GRACE

Because, Daddy. It's the right thing to do.

WYLY

The right thing is, I'll do exactly with my own goddamn horses as I goddamn please!

GRACE

Daddy. Hank's gonna ride.

WYLY

What do you think I've been doin' this for all these years? My health? Don't you have a loyal bone in your body?

GRACE

Everyone on this place is loyal to a fault. You want to win? Great. I'd love nothing more. But if you want the respect of me or anybody else in this family, you're gonna have to jump the jumps. Fair and square.

WYLY

So now you've got it figured that the stable *manager* tells the owner what to do?

GRACE

No. You don't have a stable manager anymore. I quit. I'm going back to finish vet school. I'm telling you this . . . as me.

The three of them stand silently for a moment, then WYLY heaves a huge sigh.

EMMA RAE

Come on, Grace.

They head back to the big house.

EMMA RAE

Now, doesn't that feel good?

GRACE

It really does.

WYLY
(*to himself, a smile*)

You girls . . . I swear to God.

He heads off to EMMA RAE's house.

INT. SHOW RING—LATE AFTRNOON


**VARIOUS SHOTS:**

Of the gate swinging open and the ring crew running in to change the course.

Of the red-coated ringmaster conferring with an official.

Of GEORGIA, AUNT RAE and EMMA RAE filing into the box.

INT. GATE AREA—LATE AFTERNOON

WYLY *and* JAMIE *are making last-minute adjustments, waiting to go into the ring.* WYLY *looks like a million dollars; not a trace of last night even lingers.*

> JAMIE
>
> Just stay loose. Ride it one fence at a time.

> WYLY
>
> I know.

> JAMIE
>
> I know you know but I'm sayin' it anyway!

INT. KING FARMS BOX—SHOW RING STANDS—LATE AFTERNOON

GEORGIA, AUNT RAE (*miraculously recovered*) *and* EMMA RAE *are in the box. They are dressed to the nines.* GEORGIA *is a nervous wreck. The air is taut with anticipation and every single seat in the arena is filled.*

ANNOUNCER
(*offscreen*)

Well here we are, ladies and gentlemen. Here's what we've all been waiting for. As our finalists prepare for the jump-off, our ring crew will shorten the course . . .

CAROLINE sees GRACE by the gate, and motions in sign language that she wants to come be with her. GRACE nods and signs "come on!"

CAROLINE

Daddy, can I go with Mom?

EDDIE looks at GRACE, who signs to him to send her over.

EDDIE

You want to go be with Mommy?

She nods in the affirmative.

EDDIE

Gimme a kiss. You stay with your mother . . .

INT. GATE AREA—LATE AFTERNOON

GRACE'S POINT OF VIEW *is of* EDDIE *indicating to her that* CAROLINE*'s coming.*

INT. KING FARMS BOX—LATE AFTERNOON

GEORGIA

I'll walk you halfway, Caroline.

CAROLINE and GEORGIA leave the box. EDDIE sighs.

EMMA RAE

You know, Eddie, I just had a flash.

EDDIE

I'll alert the media.

EMMA RAE

I'll bet that one day, you and Grace will make fantastic grown-ups.

INT. KING FARMS BOX——LATE AFTERNOON

GEORGIA *and* EMMA RAE *are taking their seats.* EDDIE *stands and holds their chairs like a gentleman.*

INT. SHOW RING——LATE AFTERNOON

VARIOUS SHOTS *of the female rider in the ring.*

EXT. WARM-UP RING——LATE AFTERNOON

WYLY *and* JAMIE *barely speak . . . This is the quietest* WYLY *has ever been in his life.* GRACE *and* HANK *stand quietly. They all flinch as a loud whack cracks the air. The rider in the ring has dropped a rail. As the female rider finishes, the crowd cheers.*

INT. KING FARMS BOX——NIGHT

GEORGIA *has her eyes closed in prayer.*

GEORGIA<br>(quietly)

Dear Lord, please let the right thing happen.

INT. HOLDING AREA—NIGHT

HANK *puts his foot in the stirrup and mounts Ransom while* GRACE *holds his bridle.*

> GRACE
> (*whispering to Ransom*)

You're a good boy. Give him the ride of his life.

HANK heads toward the gate as it swings open and lets the other rider out.

INT. SHOW RING—NIGHT

*We ride with* HANK *to the first obstacle, which he clears.*

INT. HOLDING AREA—NIGHT

WYLY *stands by himself, listening to* HANK*'s ride.* JAMIE *stands with Harvey, talking quietly to him.* GRACE *stands at the gate, going over every jump vicariously.*

INT. SHOW RING—NIGHT

*We ride with* HANK *as he goes over the last triple, which he clears.* HANK*'s point of view is of the digital clock with his time. A huge cheer goes up from the audience.* HANK *has a big smile and is beaming on his way toward the gate.*

INT. HOLDING AREA—NIGHT

WYLY *is on Harvey now.*

> GRACE

Good luck, Daddy.

WYLY smiles.

WYLY

No luck to it now, darlin'. Now it's all skill.

As WYLY and HANK pass each other in the gate area, WYLY says:

WYLY

Good ride, son.

INT. KING FARMS BOX—NIGHT

ANNOUNCER<br>(offscreen)

And finally number thirteen sixty-five, Have A Heart,
King Farms, James Johnson trainer and owner Wyly
King up!

Another huge cheer from the crowd as WYLY rides in, looking truly
regal on Harvey. The way he looks takes GEORGIA's breath away.

GEORGIA

Oh my God . . .

AUNT RAE sees GEORGIA's reaction and pats her arm.

AUNT RAE

It's just a man on a horse, baby girl, nothing more.
Just a man on a horse.

GEORGIA tries to be cool.

INT. SHOW RING—NIGHT

*We see* WYLY's *point of view as he checks out the course. Also* GEORGIA.

**VARIOUS SHOTS:**

Of WYLY's face, full of tense concentration, as he begins his ride.
    Of the horse's nostrils flaring heavily with effort.
    Of JAMIE by the gate watching WYLY's every move.
    Of GRACE and JAMIE catching each other's eyes and smiling slightly, tensely.
    Of GEORGIA whispering encouragement to WYLY.
    Of WYLY's point of view between the ears of Harvey.
    The excitement is really building now as WYLY has made every jump cleanly. GRACE and JAMIE trade a look. JAMIE looks about as tense as a person can possibly be.

**VARIOUS SHOTS:**

Of the digital numbers on the clock flashing by.
    Of WYLY's face as he lines up for the triple.
    Of WYLY's point of view of the clock, as he decides to push it.

**SLOW-MOTION SHOTS:**

Of Harvey as he leaves the ground for the last jump.
    Of a close-up of Harvey's back hoof as it just touches the rail, which begins to wobble.
    Of a close-up of WYLY's face as he realizes . . .
    Of a close-up of the rail as it falls, spins to the ground and lands in the dirt.
    Of HANK, who sits serene as Buddah, silently thanking God, standing as a big smile starts to spread across his face.

**RESUMING NORMAL SPEED**

GEORGIA leans down to pick up her purse. WYLY rides out of the ring.

> ANNOUNCER
>
> And that makes four disappointing faults for number thirteen sixty-five, Have A Heart. But still a win for King Farms with number fourteen thirty-four, King's Ransom becoming this year's Winter National Grand Prix Champion!!

The crowd bellows.

INT. HOLDING AREA—NIGHT

*A* CLOSE-UP *of* WYLY *in the dark. His head is bowed and his eyes are closed.* JAMIE *walks out of the backstage area, toward the barn.*

> ANNOUNCER
> (*offscreen*)
>
> Ladies and Gentlemen. Our nineteen ninety-five AMERICAN WINTER GRAND PRIX CHAMPION: KING FARMS . . . NUMBER 1434! KING'S RANSOM!! OWNER WYLY KING, RIDDEN TO VICTORY BY TRAINER HANK CORRIGAN!

HANK leads the victory gallop in the spotlight, sporting a huge grin. The entire arena is on its feet and cheering. He is the happiest man in, possibly, the world. The stands begin to empty. People congratulate GEORGIA and family.

INT. KING FARMS SHOW BARN—NIGHT

*Champagne corks are popping.* HANK *is being toasted by* DUB *and the other grooms. He takes a drink himself and offers some to Ransom.* WYLY *comes up,* all smiles, and shakes HANK's hand. GRACE comes into the barn and HANK raises his glass and then goes over and gives her a big bear hug. Hordes of people are stopping by now. They watch as CAROLINE leaps into HANK's arms and hugs him.

INT. CHANGING ROOM—NIGHT

WYLY is alone, his back to the door. He takes off his hat and dusts it off. He stands still, trying not to cry. GEORGIA comes to the door. She watches him for a moment, then goes in and closes the door behind her. She puts her hand on his shoulder which heaves with a heavy sob. He turns and they embrace tightly.

> WYLY

It's not about the horses . . .

> GEORGIA
> (soothingly)

Come on, honey. Come on home.

INT. KING HOUSE—NIGHT

The house is lit up, a band is playing in the tent and the party is in full swing.

INT. KING HOUSE—NIGHT

The foyer is candle-lit and beautiful as the family comes in. People clap and congratulate them. GRACE sees GEORGIA and WYLY arm in arm, and how incredibly happy they look, how right they are together. She and her mother exchange a glance.

INT. TENT—NIGHT

The tent is filled with white tables and chairs and is also candle-lit. A long buffet table is still full of barbecue, country ham, biscuits, etc., but the main centerpiece is a round table piled high with shrimp. WYLY, with a drink in hand, *bellows greetings to all he meets. He continuously slaps* HANK *on the back and regales all who'll listen with stories of* HANK*'s and Ransom's greatness. A really good band is playing and the dance floor is really moving.* WYLY *leads* GEORGIA *to the dance floor and they dance together like they've been doing it all their lives, which they just about have . . . and they are still in love.* CAROLINE *is on the dance floor in a group of other kids, mainly girls, doing their own interpretive style of line dance.* AUNT RAE *sits with a group of her peers. Their table is full of food and they get down to the business of eating and laughing.* EMMA RAE *comes over to* GRACE *and hands her a glass of champagne.*

EMMA RAE

Well done, sweetie.

GRACE

Thanks . . . Is that guy coming?

EMMA RAE shakes her head no.

EMMA RAE

You think I'll ever find a guy that underneath it all isn't secretly hoping I'm helpless?

GRACE kisses her on the cheek.

GRACE

It's inevitable.

They both watch their parents dancing.

EMMA RAE

That's the thing you gotta love about Daddy. Even when he loses, he wins.

They clink their champagne glasses.

EMMA RAE

To vet school.

They smile and drink.

EXT. KING HOUSE—NIGHT

WYLY *is walking through the yard toward the barn.*

INT. TRAINING BARN—NIGHT

WYLY *comes up to the door of the stall.* JAMIE *is in there alone with his horse.*

WYLY

Son . . . I guess you're right. I don't know my ass from Bakersfield. Or is it shit from shinola?

JAMIE
(*in no mood*)

Either way.

WYLY

You take him back with you. Next year, take him in there yourself. I'll pay your rate. When you're ready, I'll sell him back to you. Now, I only do 'bout one decent thing a year, so I suggest you take me up on it. Now come on up to the house and have a drink, son. You've earned at least that.

WYLY starts to leave the stall, but JAMIE doesn't move.

WYLY

Come on. Let this horse get some rest.

JAMIE comes out and heads up to the house with WYLY.

INT. TENT—NIGHT

EMMA RAE *and* CAROLINE *are dancing, with* CAROLINE *standing on the tops of* EMMA RAE*'s feet. They are really into each other right now, horse bonding.* GRACE *smiles as she watches. As* JAMIE *comes into the tent he sees* GRACE *talking to a woman.*

JAMIE

Hey. Dance later.

GRACE

Check.

JAMIE heads over to the bar and sees a grinning HANK. He goes over and shakes his hand.

JAMIE

Congratulations.

HANK

Thanks. Really.

HANK, better than anybody, understands JAMIE's disappointment.

JAMIE
(*smiling*)

I'll be glad when this goddamn year is over.

HANK

Next year, man.

INT. THE OTHER SIDE OF THE TENT—NIGHT

GRACE *is talking to* MARY JANE, *a woman from the Charity League.*

MARY JANE

Well, Grace, not to put too fine a point on it, I heard
you and Eddie were getting a divorce.

GRACE

How did you hear that?!

MARY JANE

Well, Edna told Nadine who told Kitty who told me
that she'd seen Eddie having lunch with Jack Pierce,
who is the meanest sonofabitch divorce guy in town
and you should try to hire him if Eddie hasn't because
when Betsy and Beau Barkley split—he screwed her
to the wall. I mean she got *squat!*

But GRACE is already gone. She finds EDDIE deep in one of those guy
conversations about "bidness."

GRACE

Excuse me, Eddie, I need to have a word with you for
a second. Hi, Frank, how are you.

She pulls him off to the far corner of the tent. This conversation takes
place in a furious whisper:

GRACE

Eddie! Mary Jane Reed just informed me that you and
I are getting a divorce!

EDDIE

So what, is she psychic?

GRACE

She said that you were seen having lunch with Jack
"Mad Dog" Pierce! Couldn't you be just a little more
discreet?!

EDDIE
(*sputtering*)

Discreet! You ought to be fined five hundred dollars
just for sayin' the goddamn word!

GRACE

O.K., O.K.! I just can't stand the *idea* of it being all over
the damned barbecue, it's probably in the goddamn
newspaper . . .

EDDIE

You're right! Come on. Let's go put a stop to this *right
now!*

He grabs her wrist and starts pulling her to the front of the room.
GRACE looks spooked.

GRACE

Eddie, what are you doing? Let go!

But he doesn't. He just keeps on.

EDDIE

No! Let's deal with this. Come on!

Then suddenly GRACE realizes he's taking her to the dance floor. As they're approaching the floor the bandleader says:

BANDLEADER

O.K. let's liven things up a little around here!

GRACE
(*emphatically*)

No Eddie! No!

But it's too late. The band swings into a killer soul tune and EDDIE has GRACE trapped on the dance floor. And one thing about EDDIE, the guy can cut a rug. He is a world-class shagger. He starts spinning GRACE, effortlessly, who is totally resistant. He gives her a devilish grin as he reels her back in. He does everything well, so even with GRACE trying to get away, they're the best ones on the floor. Coupled with the idea that the soon-to-be exes are dancing together, they soon have the attention of the entire party. GRACE spins in and out, up and over. When EDDIE reels her in from one spin, she says:

GRACE

I'm gonna kill you!

EDDIE
(*smiling*)

No you're not. O.K., now sweep and 'round the world . . .

They sweep and 'round the world. GRACE notices that everybody has cleared the dance floor and has formed a giant circle, with them spinning in the middle. This only enrages her further.

GRACE
(*hissing*)

This is *not* funny!

He pulls her in to walk the dog and whispers in her ear:

EDDIE

Yes it is!

And suddenly she realizes, it is. It is funny, and it's fun, and she stops resisting and they really start to wail. You can now see exactly how they were, years ago, like the pictures in the photo album. The song is almost over so EDDIE asks GRACE:

EDDIE

Up and over?

GRACE

Roger.

And he deftly puts his back to hers and flips her up and over his back, landing with a double dip. The song finishes, people are clapping. GRACE and EDDIE are looking at each other in the strangest way, hello and good-bye. If things were different, they would kiss. But they can't.

GRACE

A fitting end.

They stand with their sadness for a second.

> EDDIE
> (*quietly*)

I really am sorry.

An excited CAROLINE comes running over and grabs EDDIE's legs.

> CAROLINE

Dance with me! Dance with me!

He goes from GRACE's eyes to CAROLINE's, smiles, sweeps her up in his arms and off he goes. GRACE is left standing, panting, in the middle of the dance floor as the band starts another tune. There is a knot in her throat and her heart hurts.

WYLY waltzes over to GRACE and starts to dance with her. She is caught by surprise.

> WYLY

Bet you didn't know you still had it in you.

> GRACE

Hey Daddy.

> WYLY

Hey darlin'.

They dance for a minute while GRACE gathers her wits. For once, WYLY knows exactly what's going on. He holds her close.

> GRACE

You looked good in there tonight.

Just the slightest shadow crosses his face for a second.

> WYLY

I looked all right.

> GRACE

I was proud of you.

> WYLY

Good. I was proud of you, too.

> GRACE

Dad. I'm sorry.

> WYLY
> (*smiling*)

Don't be.

> GRACE
> (*smiling*)

I'm not.

He kisses her on the cheek and they dance away.

EDDIE and CAROLINE are dancing together. He spins her, doing a much tamer version of his dance with GRACE. CAROLINE is blissful. DISSOLVE TO:

The party has thinned way down and just the hardcore drinkers and dancers are left. GRACE sees EDDIE leave the tent and head into the house, probably to say goodnight to CAROLINE. JAMIE appears at her side.

> JAMIE

I can't dance like your husband.

GRACE

Thank God.

He and GRACE fall right into rhythm and both are a little surprised by it. They move all around the floor and JAMIE is good. GRACE lays her head on his chest and goes with it. They dance past the veranda doors, where EDDIE stands, quietly watching GRACE. WYLY comes up behind him and sees what he sees. He puts his hand on EDDIE's shoulder.

WYLY

Well son, you were lucky to get her the first time.

EDDIE

It was a damn miracle.

EDDIE turns and leaves.

EXT. KING HOUSE—NIGHT

*A* LONG SHOT *of the house with all the lights out, after the party.*

EXT. KING HOUSE—NIGHT

EDDIE *tiptoes up the front steps and carefully tries the door. It's locked.*

INT. KING HOUSE—GRACE AND EMMA RAE'S OLD BEDROOM—NIGHT

GRACE *and* EMMA RAE *lie sleeping in twin beds, in the room they shared growing up. The flowered wallpaper is covered with both paintings and photographs of horses. One wall is virtually covered with ribbons won, dating back to their early childhood.*

*Suddenly, there's a tapping sound.* EMMA RAE *wakes up and goes to the window. She sees nothing but hears a thump. She opens the window and sticks her head out.* EMMA RAE*'s point of view is of* EDDIE *clinging to the slippery roof.* EMMA RAE *closes the window.*

> EDDIE
>
> Please, Em . . . just this once, show some mercy.

She opens the window again and extends her hand.

> EMMA RAE
>
> Come on, Ed. If I thought you were a total piece of shit, I wouldn't bother giving you such a hard time.

EDDIE grabs EMMA RAE's hand. She helps him climb into the room. GRACE is still sound asleep. EDDIE huffs and puffs his way to his feet.

> EDDIE
>
> That's not as easy as it used to be.

> EMMA RAE
>
> What is.

Suddenly, a scream. It's GRACE. EDDIE screams, scaring EMMA RAE. She screams.

> EVERYBODY
> (*furious whispers*)
>
> Quiet! You scared the living daylights out of me! Will you cut that out?

Everyone freezes and listens for stirrings in the house. Finally, EMMA RAE breaks the silence.

EMMA RAE

Well, I'm gonna go see a horse about a man . . .

EMMA RAE slips out of the room. EDDIE approaches GRACE's bed and tentatively sits down.

EDDIE

I have to talk to you. Grace, I had fun tonight.

GRACE

Me too.

EDDIE leans in close, his eyes full of longing.

EDDIE

Grace, remember when I said that when I asked you to marry me, I didn't think you'd say yes? (GRACE *waits*.) I hoped that you would.

GRACE
(*tenderly*)

I know.

EDDIE

Grace . . . if I could go back . . . if we could get back to where we were before, *I would go!* Would you?

GRACE

I don't know. It's like . . . how would we make sure we didn't end up right back here?

EDDIE

I'd be different. I'd talk to you before it was too late
. . . I wouldn't do things you can't take back.

GRACE

It's not just about that! It's my fault too, and I'm sorry.
But I want to be different, too. I just don't want to
come to the end of my life and have to say *"I was gonna
be different* but I chickened out when I had the chance."
And this is it Eddie, this is my opportunity to become
someone that I can be proud of, and I don't want to
blow it.

EDDIE embraces her and presses his face into her hair and breathes
her in. They really hug.

EDDIE

All right. I'm gonna go. You and Caroline move back
home. O.K.? I'll get a place . . . It's better for her.

GRACE

O.K.

EDDIE

I love you, Grace.

GRACE

I love you, too.

He gets up. GRACE watches him cross the room to the window.

GRACE
(*whispering*)

Eddie . . . you can use the door.

EDDIE leaves.

EXT. KING FARMS TRAINING BARN—DAY

*A* LONG SHOT *of* CAROLINE *and* GRACE *riding bareback around the field. The day is overcast. All the awnings are down from the barn, the trailers are mostly gone. The place feels somewhat deserted.*

JAMIE*'s truck and trailer are parked at one end of the barn.* DUB *and another groom load Harvey into the trailer and close the gate.* HANK *and* JAMIE *shake hands and make jokes.*

GRACE *sees that* JAMIE *is about to leave. She rides over and hops off the horse, as* CAROLINE *continues to ride around.* GRACE *and* JAMIE *walk to the door of* JAMIE*'s truck.*

GRACE

I'll bet you're glad to be rollin' out of here.

JAMIE

It's been . . . interesting.

They smile. They watch CAROLINE. They look at each other.

JAMIE

I'll see you next year.

GRACE

I'll be here.

It's almost like he doesn't want to leave. They smile. They hug each other good-bye.

JAMIE

Maybe in another life, huh?

GRACE
(*smiling*)

You never know. This life's not over yet.

He climbs into the cab and starts it up. GRACE watches as he rolls out of the driveway. CAROLINE rides along the fence waving to him. He smiles and blows her a kiss. GRACE watches the trailer disappear down the road. CAROLINE rides up to GRACE. She scoots forward on the horse and GRACE hops up onto Peach's back.

EXT. SCHOOL OF VETERINARY MEDICINE—LATE AFTERNOON

GRACE *emerges from the building and is rushing down the steps, loaded with books. Her friend* LIZ *catches up to her.*

LIZ

Hey, Grace, I'm meeting Melissa for ribs later. You wanna come? Bring Caroline.

GRACE

Sorry. Can't. Got a date.

LIZ

A date? Or a "date" date?

GRACE
(*smiling*)

A first date . . .

They wave good-bye and head off in different directions.

EXT. STREET—EVENING

GRACE *pulls up in front of her house and goes inside.*

INT. GRACE'S HOUSE—EVENING

GRACE *enters. She hears the buzz of a Cuisinart and follows the sound down the hallway to the kitchen.* EDDIE *is standing with his back to her, poring over a cookbook, knife in hand. He didn't hear her come in, but he senses someone.*

EDDIE

Grace?

He turns around. There she is in the doorway. They smile at each other.

GRACE

Hi.

EDDIE

Hi. How was school?

GRACE

Great. You're early.

EDDIE

I know. Caroline let me in. I hope you don't mind.

GRACE

No, it's fine. It looks like a cooking show in here.

And it does too. Everything is chopped and in little bowls, eggs are separated, etc. . . .

EDDIE

Well, hey, you finally say yes to dinner, I figured it better be good.

GRACE

Wow . . . poached pears?

EDDIE

. . . with a Chantilly cream.

He points to the Cuisinart. GRACE is impressed. She goes over and sticks her finger in the Chantilly cream. She starts to taste it, hesitates, smiles . . . and holds out her finger to EDDIE . . .

GRACE

You first . . .

A SLOW-MOTION SHOT: EDDIE smiles, hesitates briefly and licks it off her finger. They both laugh as we . . .

**FADE TO BLACK OVER MUSIC.**